Dynamite Entertainment Presents

P9-CQH-857

The BOYS ™
HIGHLAND LADDIE

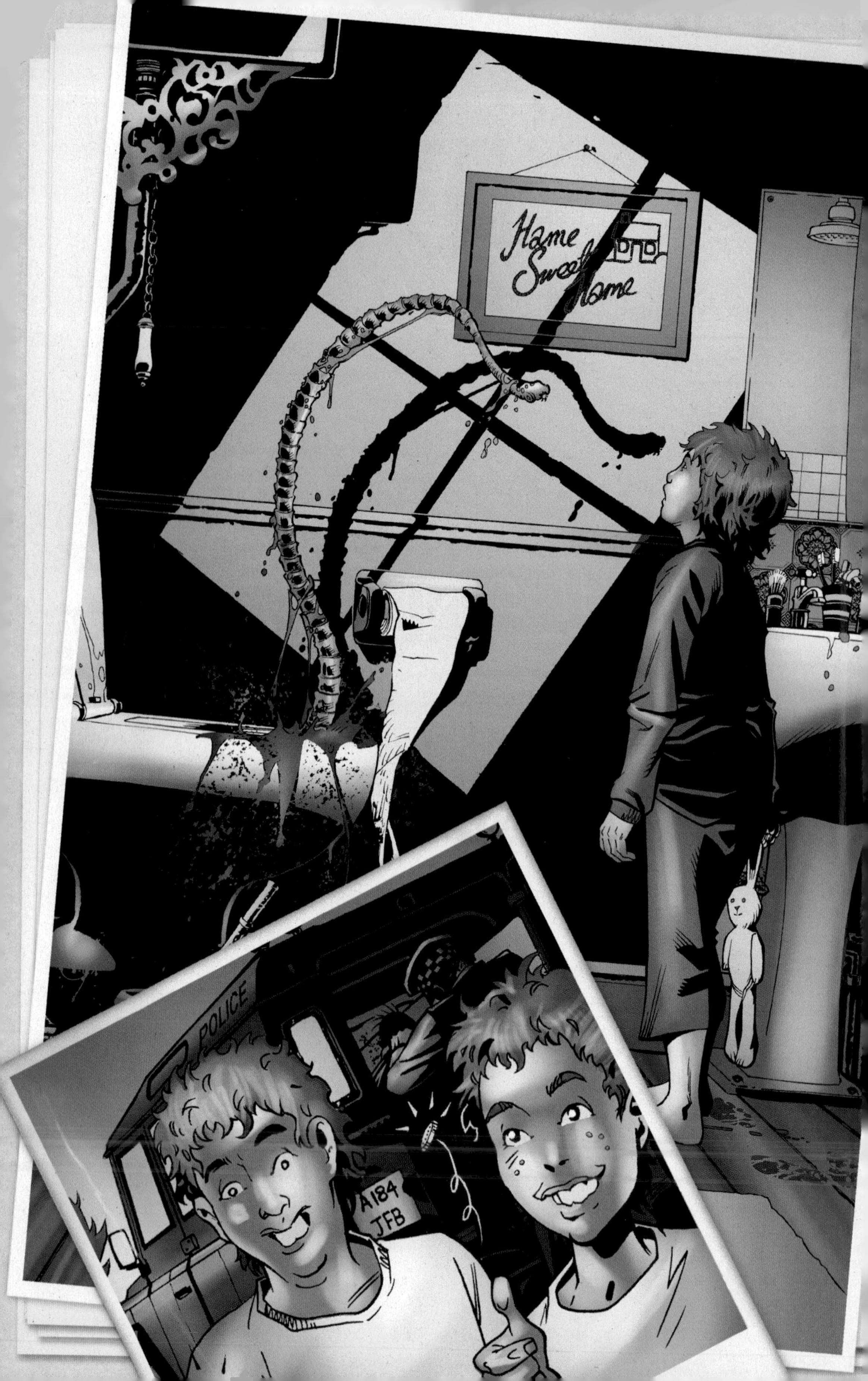
Home Sweet Home
POLICE
A184 JFB

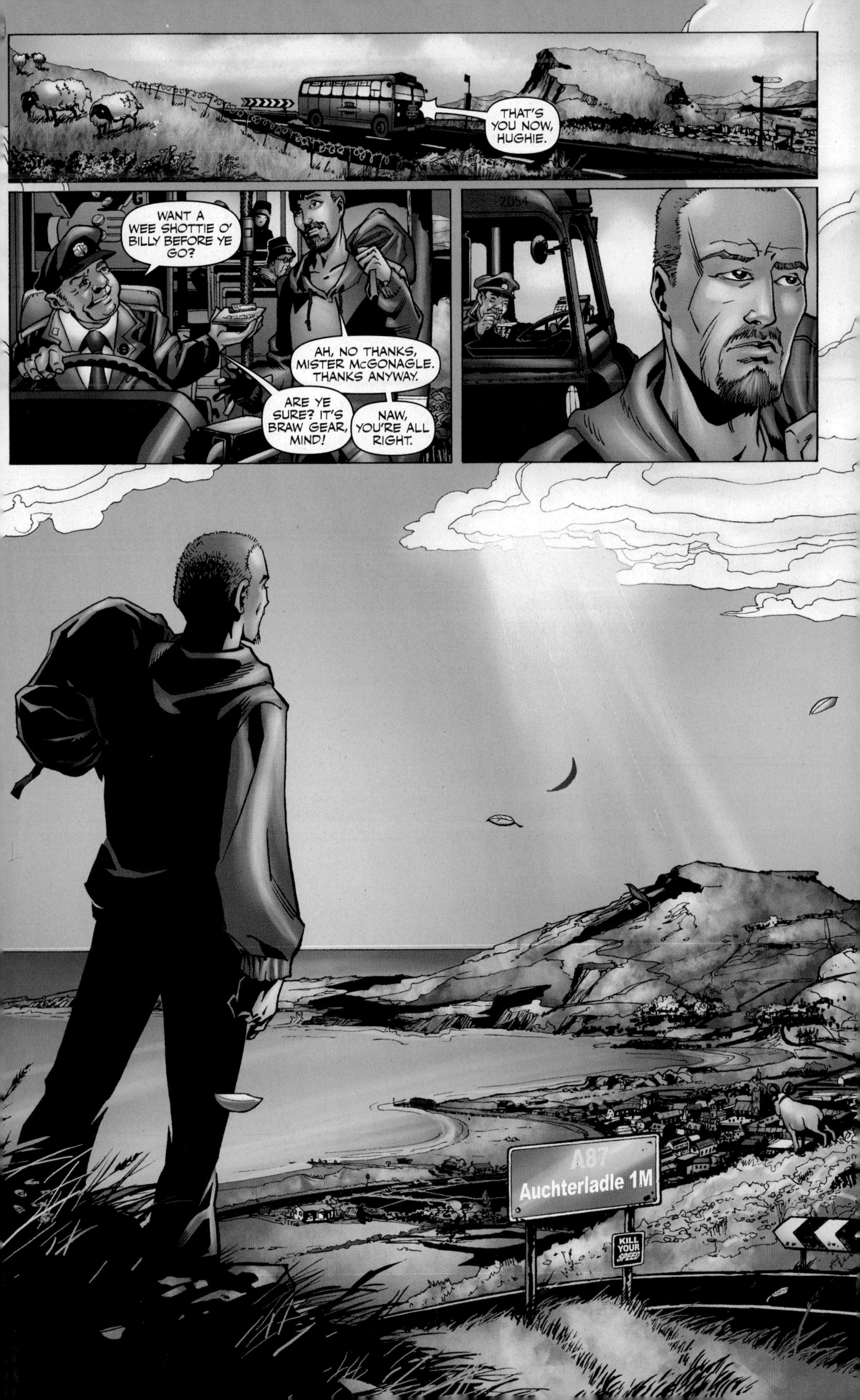
THAT'S YOU NOW, HUGHIE.
WANT A WEE SHOTTIE O' BILLY BEFORE YE GO?
AH, NO THANKS, MISTER McGONAGLE. THANKS ANYWAY.
ARE YE SURE? IT'S BRAW GEAR, MIND!
NAW, YOU'RE ALL RIGHT.
A87
Auchterladle 1M
KILL YOUR SPEED

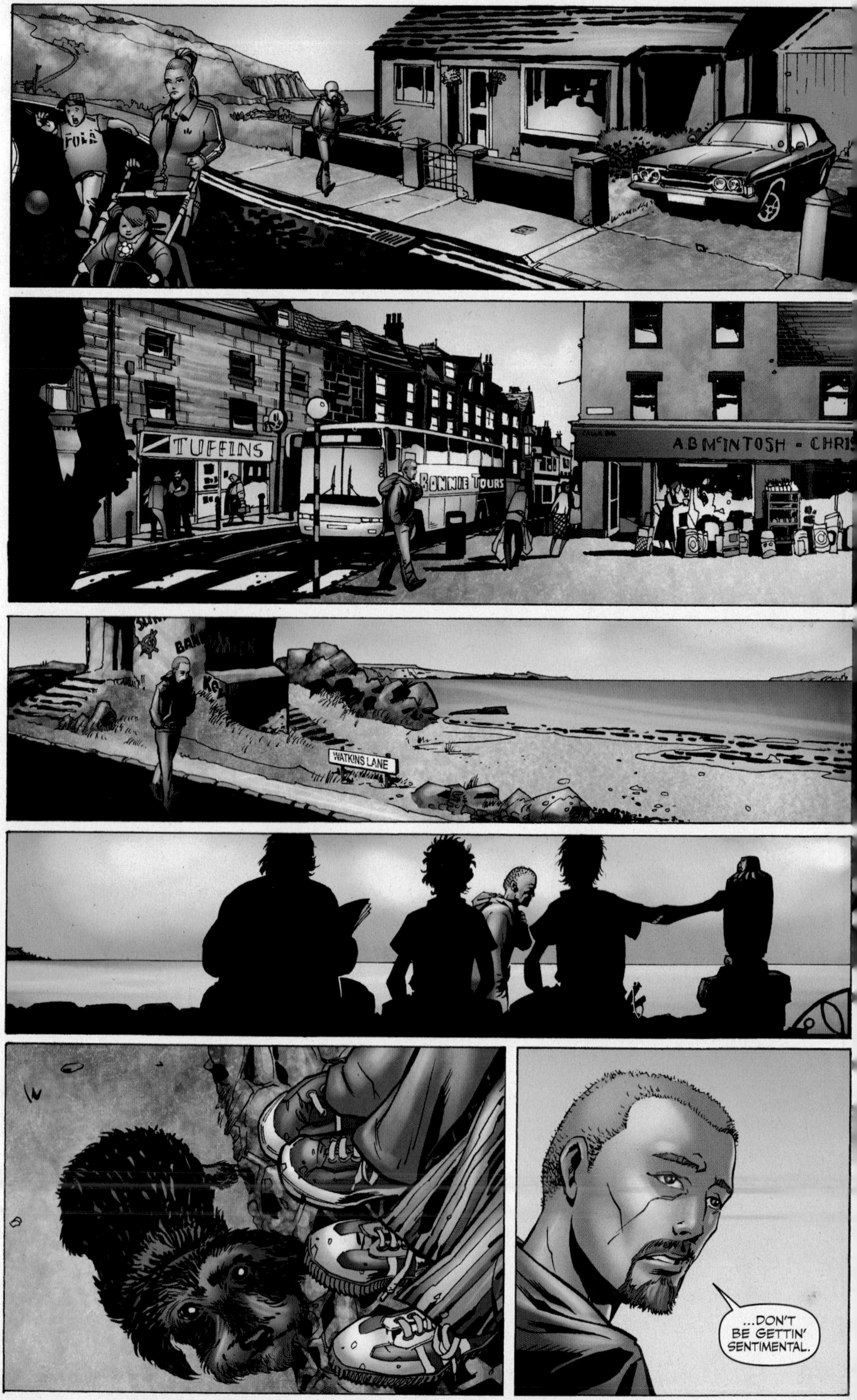
FOLA
TUFFINS
BONNIE TOURS
A.B. McINTOSH - CHRIS
WATKINS LANE
...DON'T BE GETTIN' SENTIMENTAL.

one

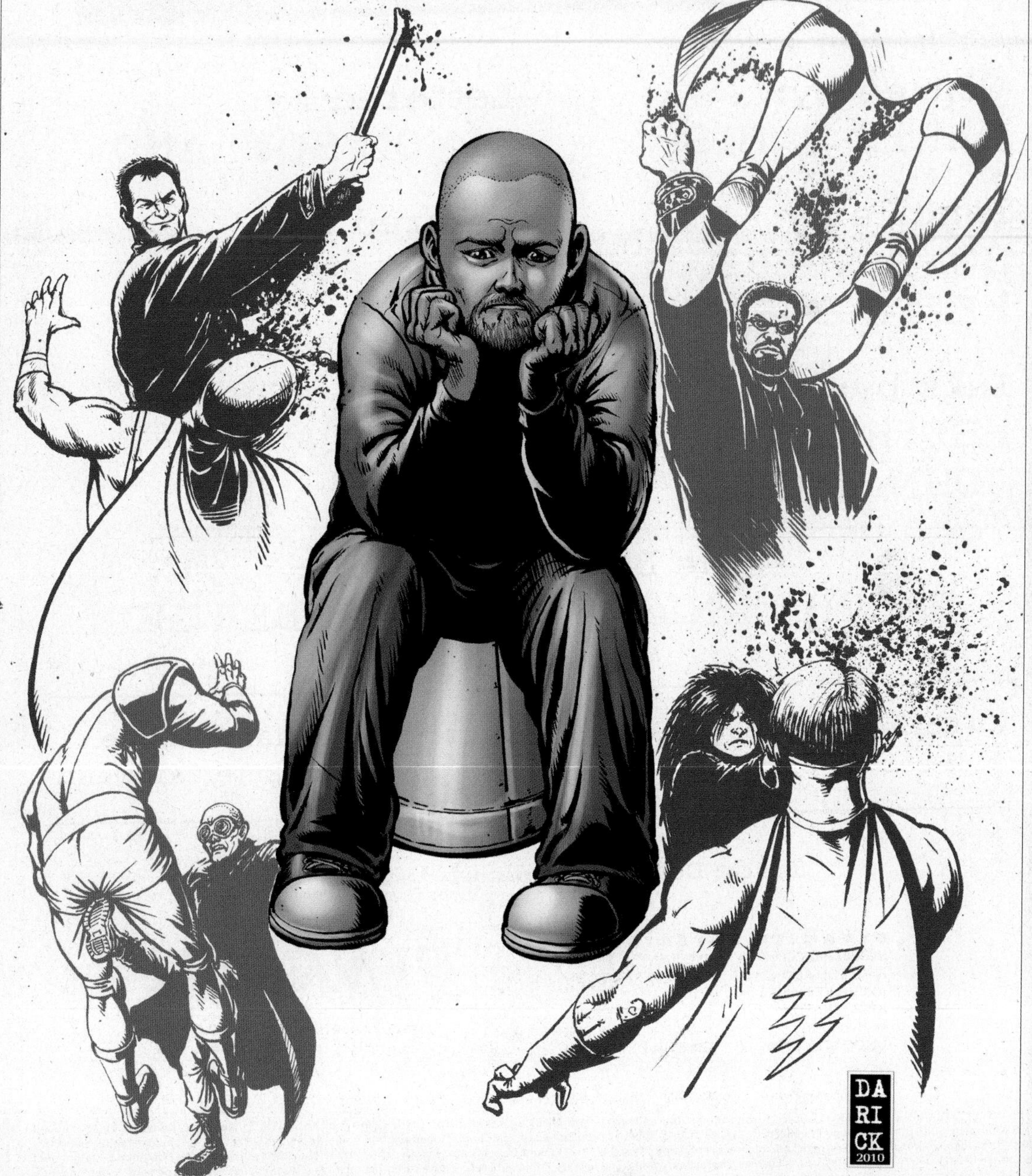
DA
RI
CK
2010

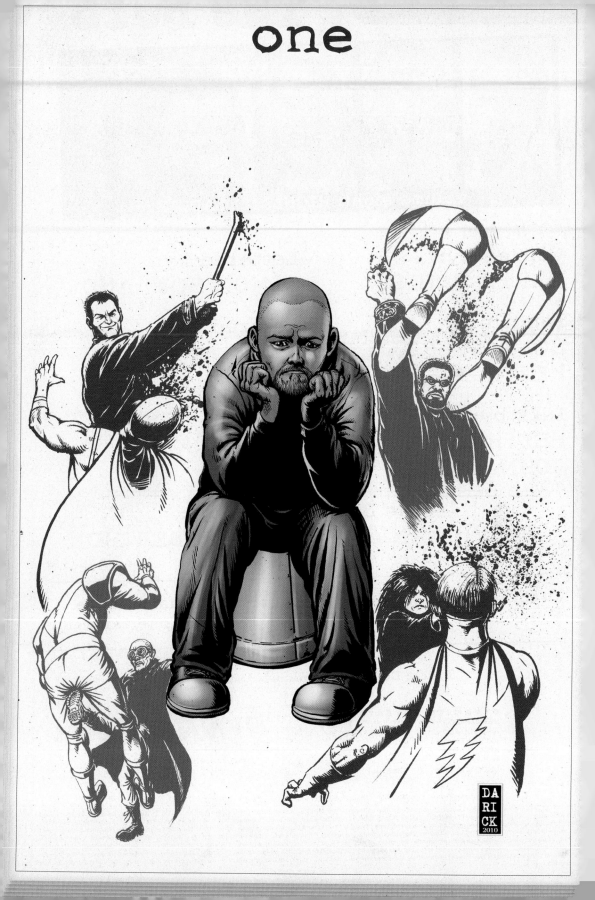

volume eight: HIGHLAND LADDIE

Written by:
GARTH ENNIS

Pencils by:
JOHN McCREA w/ KEITH BURNS

Inks by:
KEITH BURNS w/ JOHN McCREA

Lettered by:
SIMON BOWLAND

Colored by:
TONY AVIÑA

Covers by:
DARICK ROBERTSON & TONY AVIÑA

The Boys created by:
GARTH ENNIS & DARICK ROBERTSON

Collects issues one through six of the Highland Laddie mini-series, originally published by Dynamite Entertainment.

Trade Design by: JASON ULLMEYER

DYNAMITE ENTERTAINMENT
NICK BARRUCCI • PRESIDENT
JUAN COLLADO • CHIEF OPERATING OFFICER
JOSEPH RYBANDT • EDITOR
JOSH JOHNSON • CREATIVE DIRECTOR
RICH YOUNG • BUSINESS DEVELOPMENT
JASON ULLMEYER • GRAPHIC DESIGNER

DYNAMITE
ENTERTAINMENT
WWW.DYNAMITEENTERTAINMENT.COM

Softcover ISBN-10: 1-60690-207-5   Softcover ISBN-13: 978-1-60690-207-3   First Printing   10 9 8 7 6 5 4 3 2 1

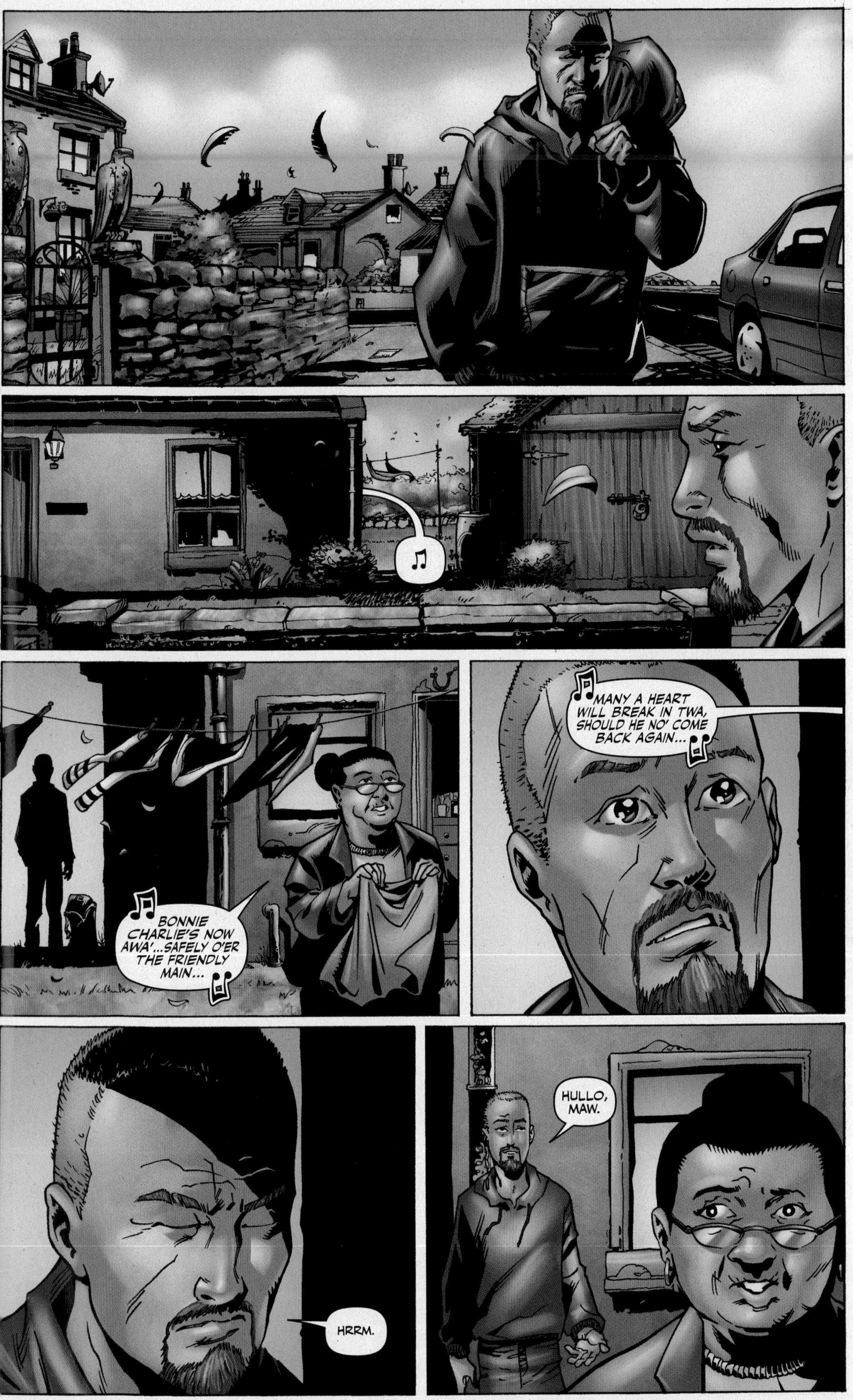
♫
BONNIE CHARLIE'S NOW AWA'...SAFELY O'ER THE FRIENDLY MAIN...
MANY A HEART WILL BREAK IN TWA, SHOULD HE NO' COME BACK AGAIN...
HRRM.
HULLO, MAW.

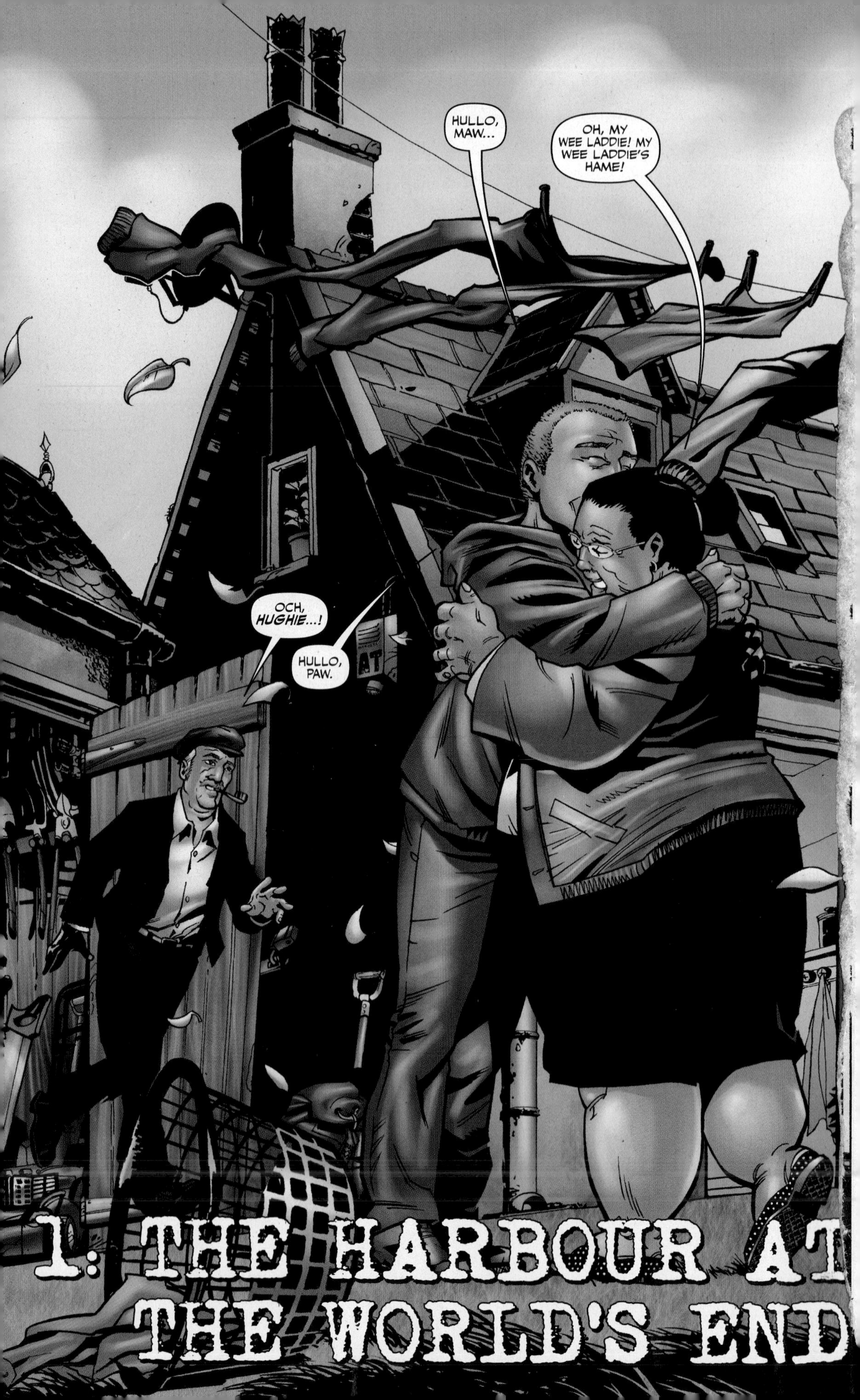
HULLO, MAW...
OH, MY WEE LADDIE! MY WEE LADDIE'S HAME!
OCH, HUGHIE...!
HULLO, PAW.
1: THE HARBOUR AT THE WORLD'S END

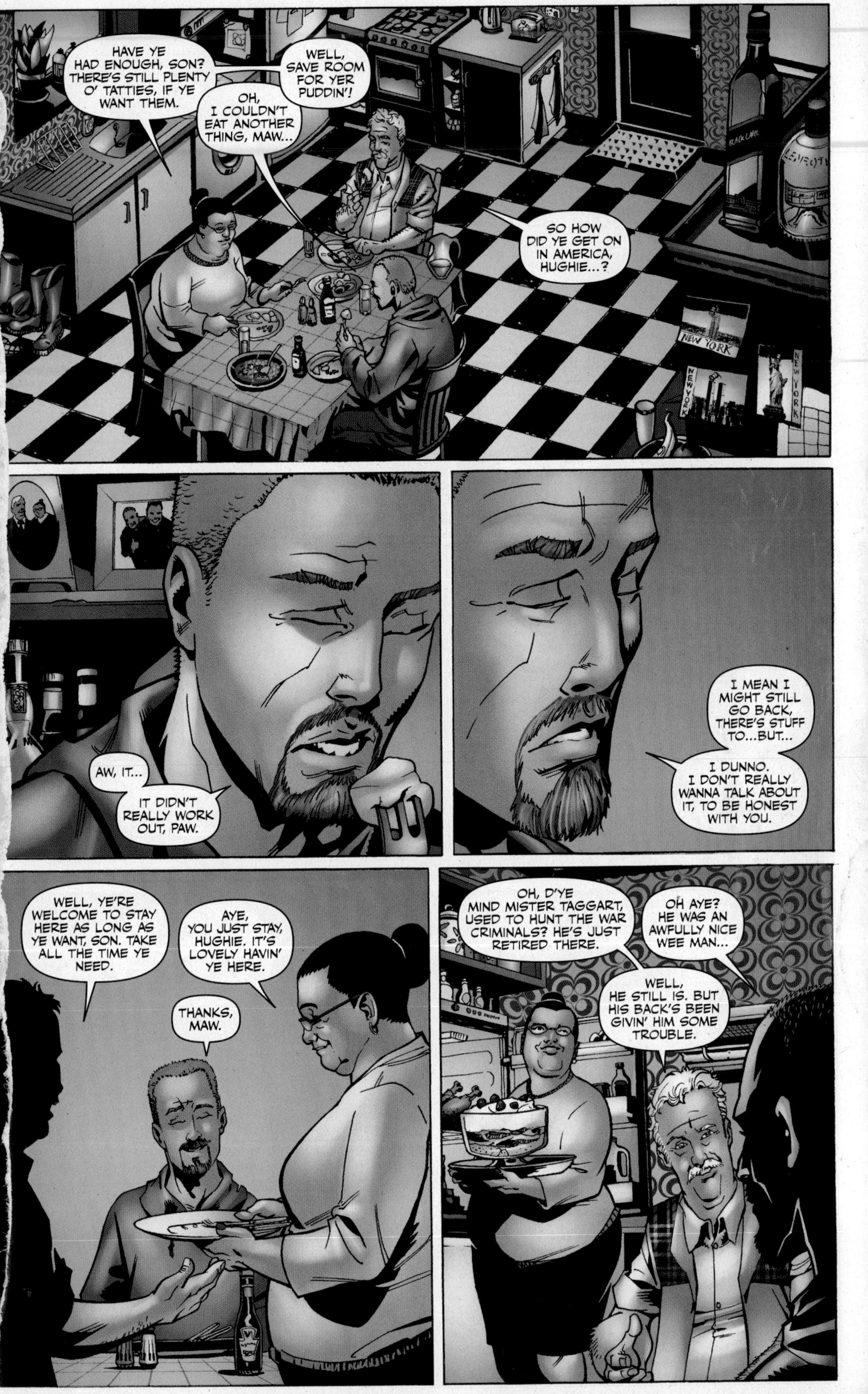
HAVE YE HAD ENOUGH, SON? THERE'S STILL PLENTY O' TATTIES, IF YE WANT THEM.
WELL, SAVE ROOM FOR YER PUDDIN'!
OH, I COULDN'T EAT ANOTHER THING, MAW...
SO HOW DID YE GET ON IN AMERICA, HUGHIE...?
BLACK LABEL
NEW YORK
NEW YORK
NEW YORK
AW, IT...
IT DIDN'T REALLY WORK OUT, PAW.
I MEAN I MIGHT STILL GO BACK, THERE'S STUFF TO...BUT...
I DUNNO. I DON'T REALLY WANNA TALK ABOUT IT, TO BE HONEST WITH YOU.
WELL, YE'RE WELCOME TO STAY HERE AS LONG AS YE WANT, SON. TAKE ALL THE TIME YE NEED.
AYE, YOU JUST STAY, HUGHIE. IT'S LOVELY HAVIN' YE HERE.
THANKS, MAW.
OH, D'YE MIND MISTER TAGGART, USED TO HUNT THE WAR CRIMINALS? HE'S JUST RETIRED THERE.
OH AYE? HE WAS AN AWFULLY NICE WEE MAN...
WELL, HE STILL IS. BUT HIS BACK'S BEEN GIVIN' HIM SOME TROUBLE.

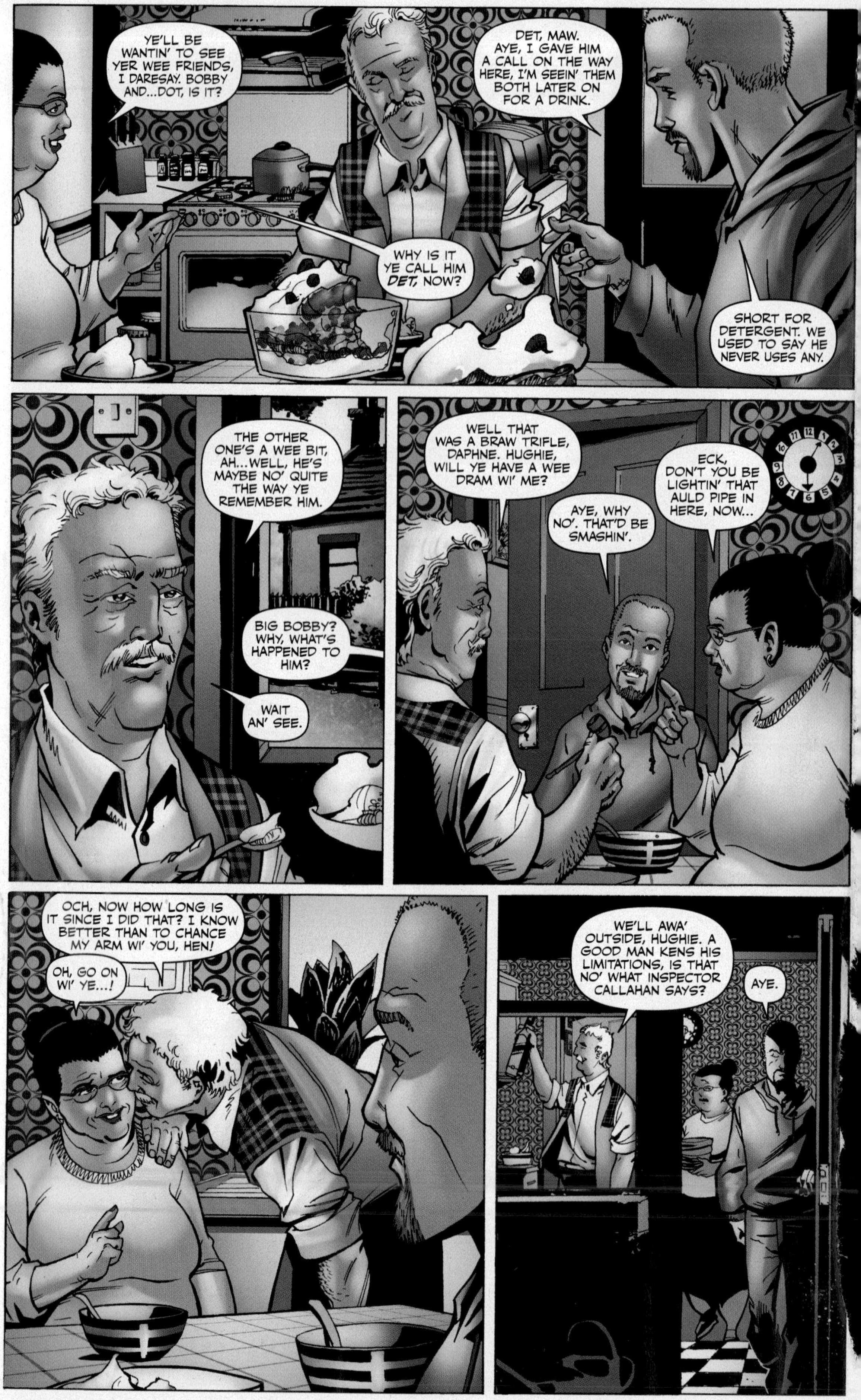
YE'LL BE WANTIN' TO SEE YER WEE FRIENDS, I DARESAY. BOBBY AND...DOT, IS IT?
DET, MAW. AYE, I GAVE HIM A CALL ON THE WAY HERE, I'M SEEIN' THEM BOTH LATER ON FOR A DRINK.
WHY IS IT YE CALL HIM DET, NOW?
SHORT FOR DETERGENT. WE USED TO SAY HE NEVER USES ANY.
THE OTHER ONE'S A WEE BIT, AH...WELL, HE'S MAYBE NO' QUITE THE WAY YE REMEMBER HIM.
BIG BOBBY? WHY, WHAT'S HAPPENED TO HIM?
WAIT AN' SEE.
WELL THAT WAS A BRAW TRIFLE, DAPHNE. HUGHIE, WILL YE HAVE A WEE DRAM WI' ME?
AYE, WHY NO'. THAT'D BE SMASHIN'.
ECK, DON'T YOU BE LIGHTIN' THAT AULD PIPE IN HERE, NOW...
OCH, NOW HOW LONG IS IT SINCE I DID THAT? I KNOW BETTER THAN TO CHANCE MY ARM WI' YOU, HEN!
OH, GO ON WI' YE...!
WE'LL AWA' OUTSIDE, HUGHIE. A GOOD MAN KENS HIS LIMITATIONS, IS THAT NO' WHAT INSPECTOR CALLAHAN SAYS?
AYE.

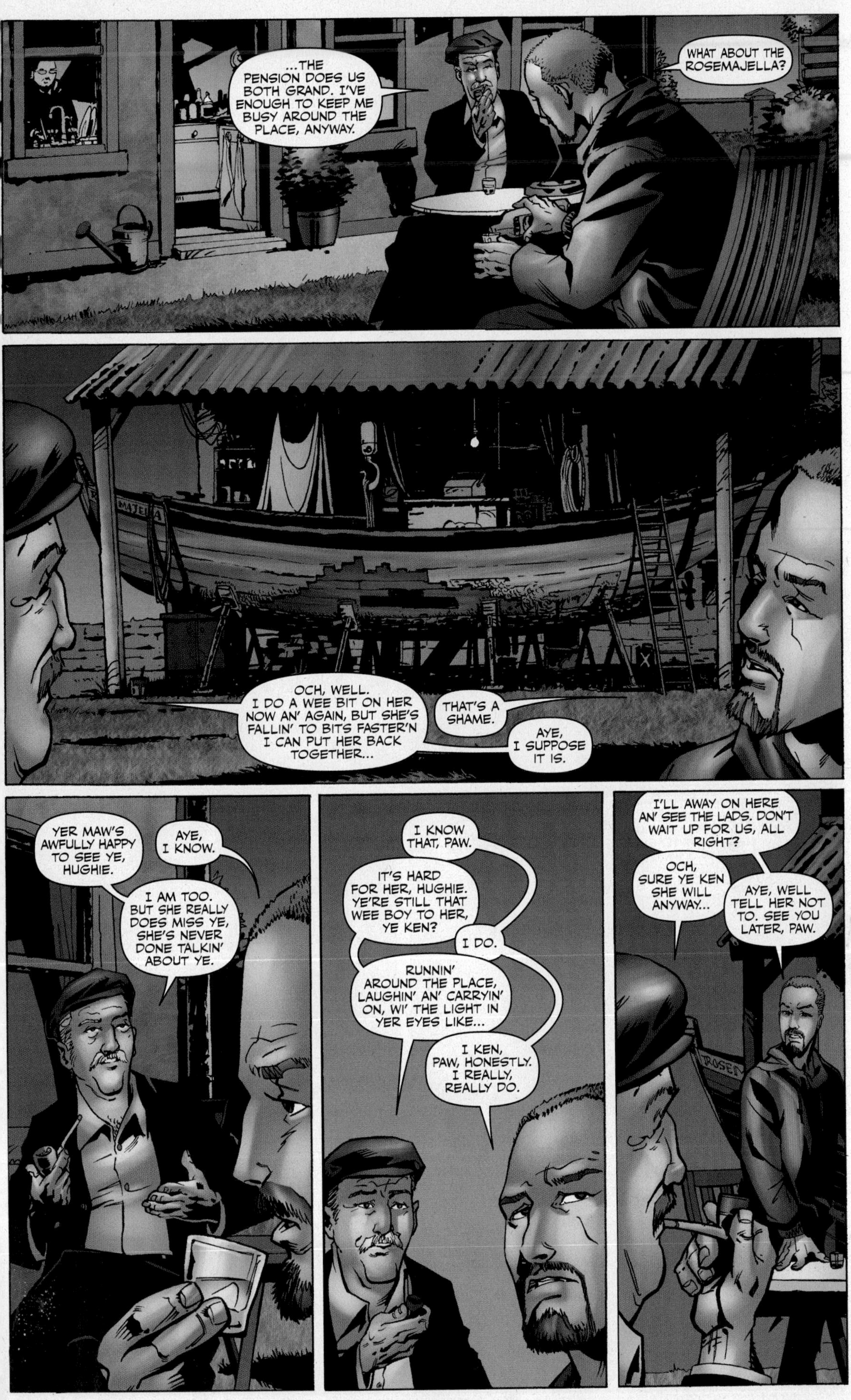
...THE PENSION DOES US BOTH GRAND. I'VE ENOUGH TO KEEP ME BUSY AROUND THE PLACE, ANYWAY.
WHAT ABOUT THE ROSEMAJELLA?
OCH, WELL. I DO A WEE BIT ON HER NOW AN' AGAIN, BUT SHE'S FALLIN' TO BITS FASTER'N I CAN PUT HER BACK TOGETHER...
THAT'S A SHAME.
AYE, I SUPPOSE IT IS.
YER MAW'S AWFULLY HAPPY TO SEE YE, HUGHIE.
AYE, I KNOW.
I AM TOO. BUT SHE REALLY DOES MISS YE, SHE'S NEVER DONE TALKIN' ABOUT YE.
I KNOW THAT, PAW.
IT'S HARD FOR HER, HUGHIE. YE'RE STILL THAT WEE BOY TO HER, YE KEN?
I DO.
RUNNIN' AROUND THE PLACE, LAUGHIN' AN' CARRYIN' ON, WI' THE LIGHT IN YER EYES LIKE...
I KEN, PAW, HONESTLY. I REALLY, REALLY DO.
I'LL AWAY ON HERE AN' SEE THE LADS. DON'T WAIT UP FOR US, ALL RIGHT?
OCH, SURE YE KEN SHE WILL ANYWAY...
AYE, WELL TELL HER NOT TO. SEE YOU LATER, PAW.

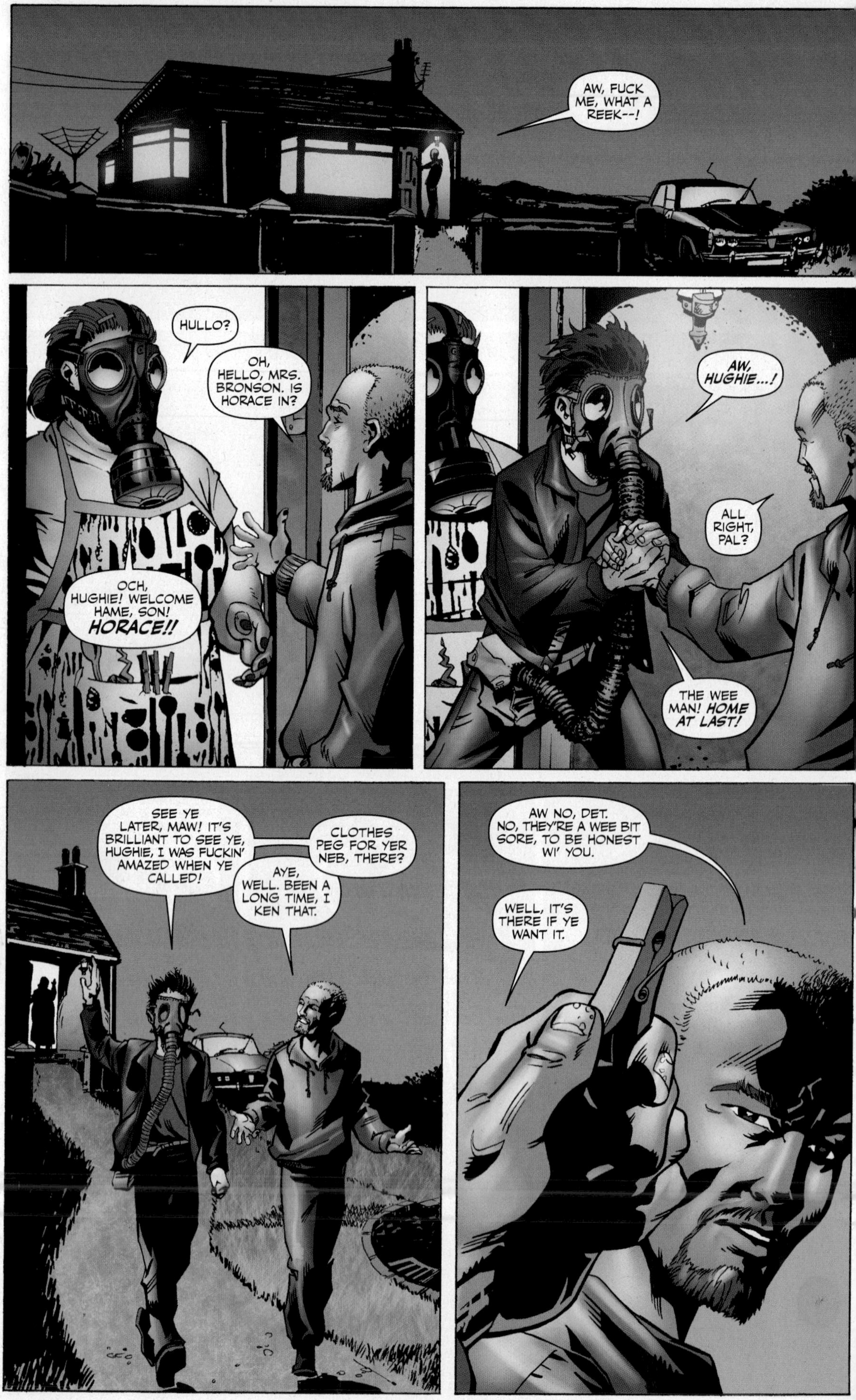
AW, FUCK ME, WHAT A REEK--!
HULLO?
OH, HELLO, MRS. BRONSON. IS HORACE IN?
OCH, HUGHIE! WELCOME HAME, SON! HORACE!!
AW, HUGHIE...!
ALL RIGHT, PAL?
THE WEE MAN! HOME AT LAST!
SEE YE LATER, MAW! IT'S BRILLIANT TO SEE YE, HUGHIE, I WAS FUCKIN' AMAZED WHEN YE CALLED!
AYE, WELL. BEEN A LONG TIME, I KEN THAT.
CLOTHES PEG FOR YER NEB, THERE?
AW NO, DET. NO, THEY'RE A WEE BIT SORE, TO BE HONEST WI' YOU.
WELL, IT'S THERE IF YE WANT IT.

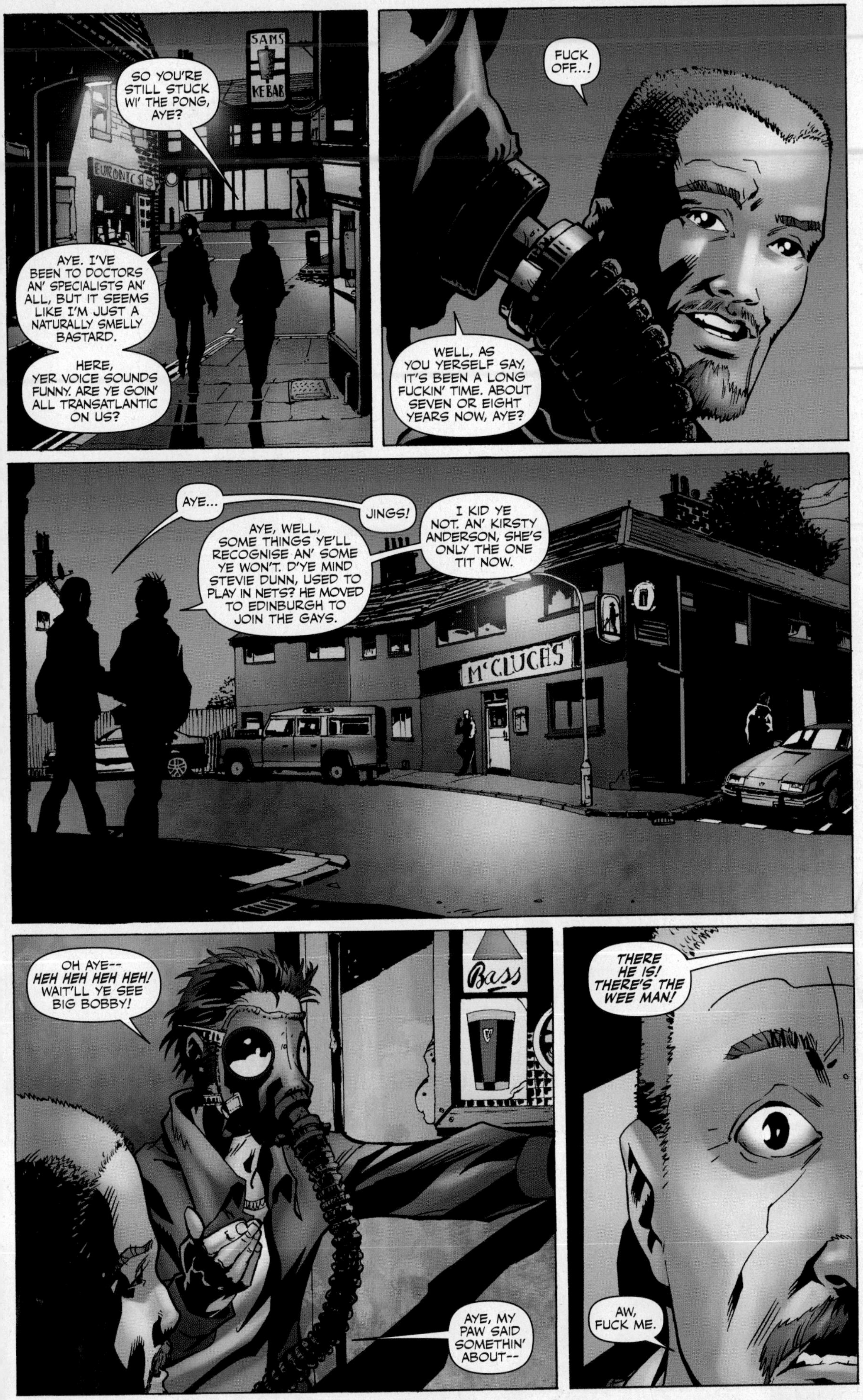
SAMS KEBAB
EURONICS
SO YOU'RE STILL STUCK WI' THE PONG, AYE?
AYE. I'VE BEEN TO DOCTORS AN' SPECIALISTS AN' ALL, BUT IT SEEMS LIKE I'M JUST A NATURALLY SMELLY BASTARD.
HERE, YER VOICE SOUNDS FUNNY. ARE YE GOIN' ALL TRANSATLANTIC ON US?
FUCK OFF...!
WELL, AS YOU YERSELF SAY, IT'S BEEN A LONG FUCKIN' TIME. ABOUT SEVEN OR EIGHT YEARS NOW, AYE?
AYE...
AYE, WELL, SOME THINGS YE'LL RECOGNISE AN' SOME YE WON'T. D'YE MIND STEVIE DUNN, USED TO PLAY IN NETS? HE MOVED TO EDINBURGH TO JOIN THE GAYS.
JINGS!
I KID YE NOT. AN' KIRSTY ANDERSON, SHE'S ONLY THE ONE TIT NOW.
McCLUCAS
OH AYE-- *HEH HEH HEH HEH!* WAIT'LL YE SEE BIG BOBBY!
Bass
AYE, MY PAW SAID SOMETHIN' ABOUT--
THERE HE IS! THERE'S THE WEE MAN!
AW, FUCK ME.

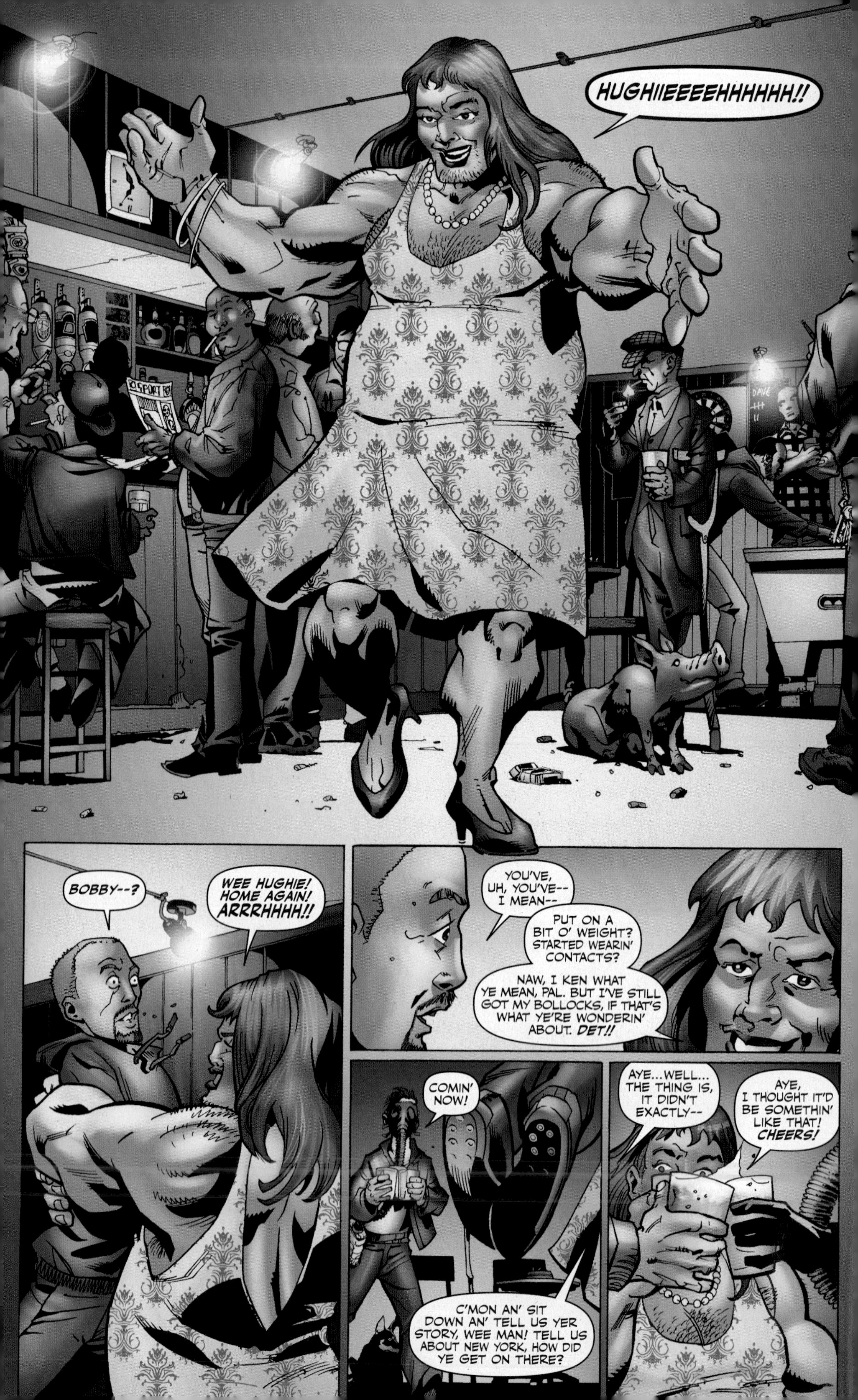
HUGHIIEEEEHHHHHH!!
SPORT
DAVE
BOBBY--?
WEE HUGHIE! HOME AGAIN! ARRRHHHH!!
YOU'VE, UH, YOU'VE-- I MEAN--
PUT ON A BIT O' WEIGHT? STARTED WEARIN' CONTACTS?
NAW, I KEN WHAT YE MEAN, PAL. BUT I'VE STILL GOT MY BOLLOCKS, IF THAT'S WHAT YE'RE WONDERIN' ABOUT. DET!!
COMIN' NOW!
C'MON AN' SIT DOWN AN' TELL US YER STORY, WEE MAN! TELL US ABOUT NEW YORK, HOW DID YE GET ON THERE?
AYE...WELL... THE THING IS, IT DIDN'T EXACTLY--
AYE, I THOUGHT IT'D BE SOMETHIN' LIKE THAT! CHEERS!

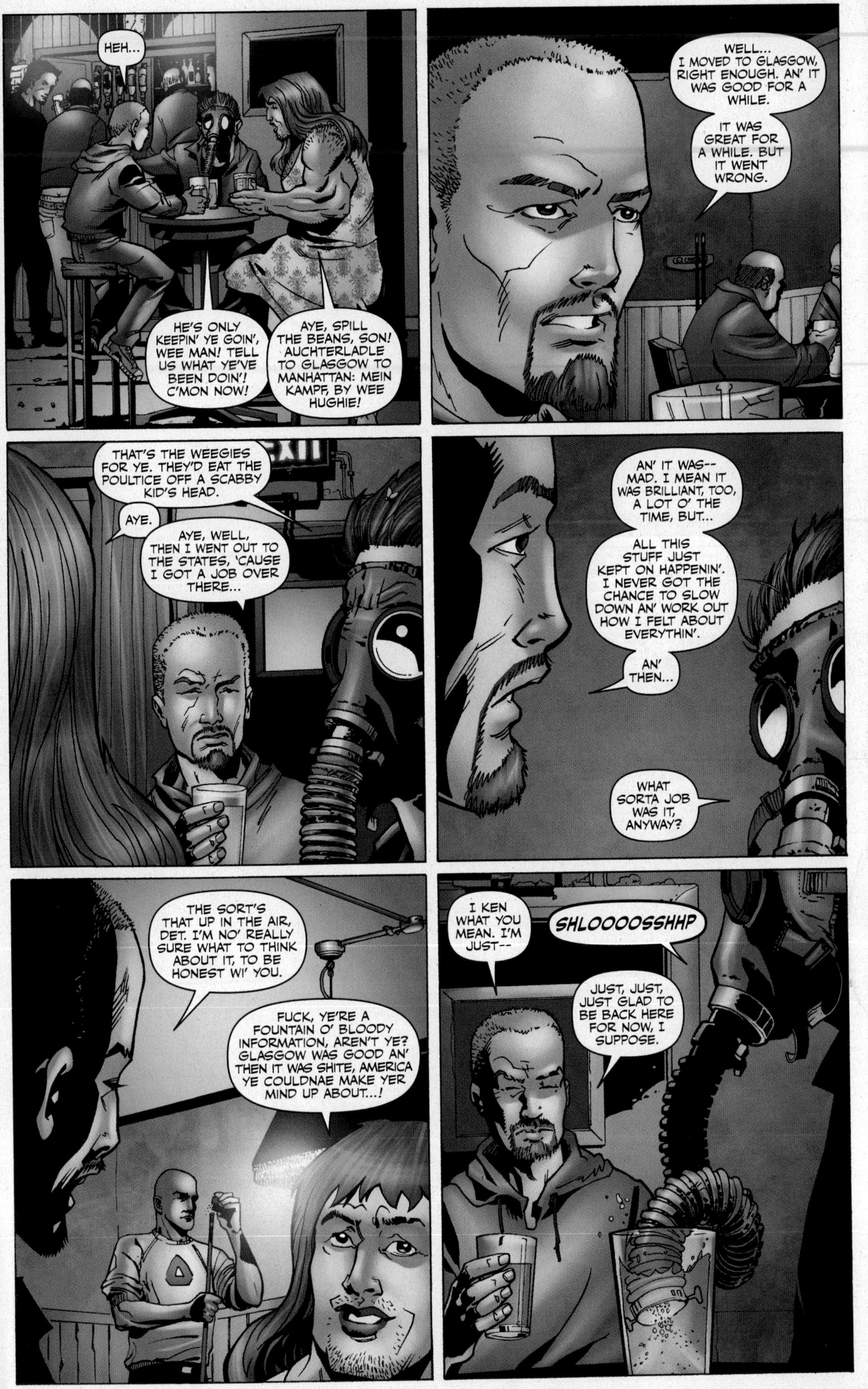
HEH...
HE'S ONLY KEEPIN' YE GOIN', WEE MAN! TELL US WHAT YE'VE BEEN DOIN'! C'MON NOW!
AYE, SPILL THE BEANS, SON! AUCHTERLADLE TO GLASGOW TO MANHATTAN: MEIN KAMPF, BY WEE HUGHIE!
WELL... I MOVED TO GLASGOW, RIGHT ENOUGH. AN' IT WAS GOOD FOR A WHILE.
IT WAS GREAT FOR A WHILE. BUT IT WENT WRONG.
THAT'S THE WEEGIES FOR YE. THEY'D EAT THE POULTICE OFF A SCABBY KID'S HEAD.
AYE.
AYE, WELL, THEN I WENT OUT TO THE STATES, 'CAUSE I GOT A JOB OVER THERE...
AN' IT WAS-- MAD. I MEAN IT WAS BRILLIANT, TOO, A LOT O' THE TIME, BUT...
ALL THIS STUFF JUST KEPT ON HAPPENIN'. I NEVER GOT THE CHANCE TO SLOW DOWN AN' WORK OUT HOW I FELT ABOUT EVERYTHIN'.
AN' THEN...
WHAT SORTA JOB WAS IT, ANYWAY?
THE SORT'S THAT UP IN THE AIR, DET. I'M NO' REALLY SURE WHAT TO THINK ABOUT IT, TO BE HONEST WI' YOU.
FUCK, YE'RE A FOUNTAIN O' BLOODY INFORMATION, AREN'T YE? GLASGOW WAS GOOD AN' THEN IT WAS SHITE, AMERICA YE COULDNAE MAKE YER MIND UP ABOUT...!
I KEN WHAT YOU MEAN. I'M JUST--
SHLOOOOSSHHP
JUST, JUST, JUST GLAD TO BE BACK HERE FOR NOW, I SUPPOSE.

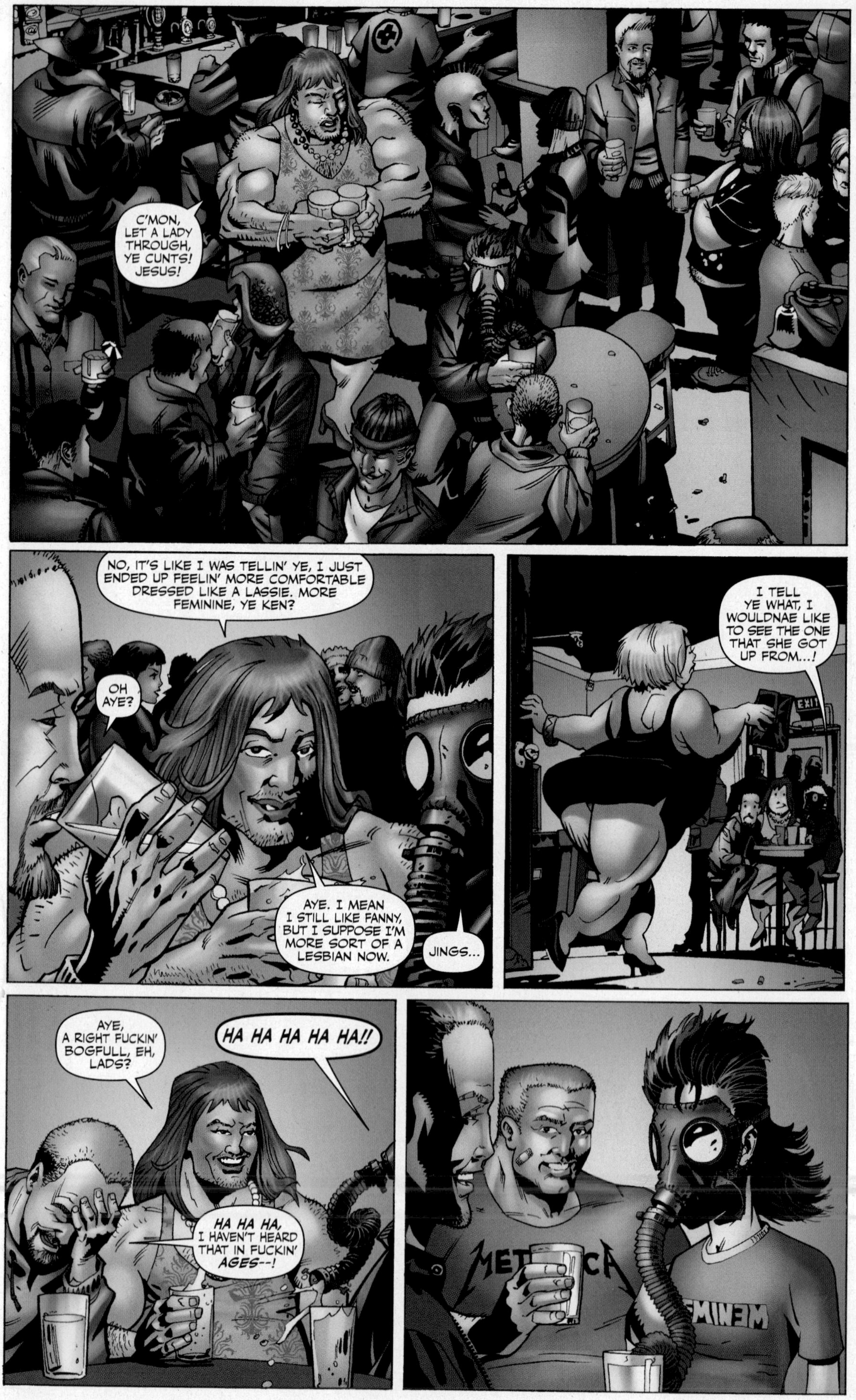
C'MON, LET A LADY THROUGH, YE CUNTS! JESUS!
NO, IT'S LIKE I WAS TELLIN' YE, I JUST ENDED UP FEELIN' MORE COMFORTABLE DRESSED LIKE A LASSIE. MORE FEMININE, YE KEN?
OH AYE?
AYE. I MEAN I STILL LIKE FANNY, BUT I SUPPOSE I'M MORE SORT OF A LESBIAN NOW.
JINGS...
I TELL YE WHAT, I WOULDNAE LIKE TO SEE THE ONE THAT SHE GOT UP FROM...!
EXIT
AYE, A RIGHT FUCKIN' BOGFULL, EH, LADS?
HA HA HA HA HA!!
HA HA HA, I HAVEN'T HEARD THAT IN FUCKIN' AGES--!
METALLICA
EMINEM

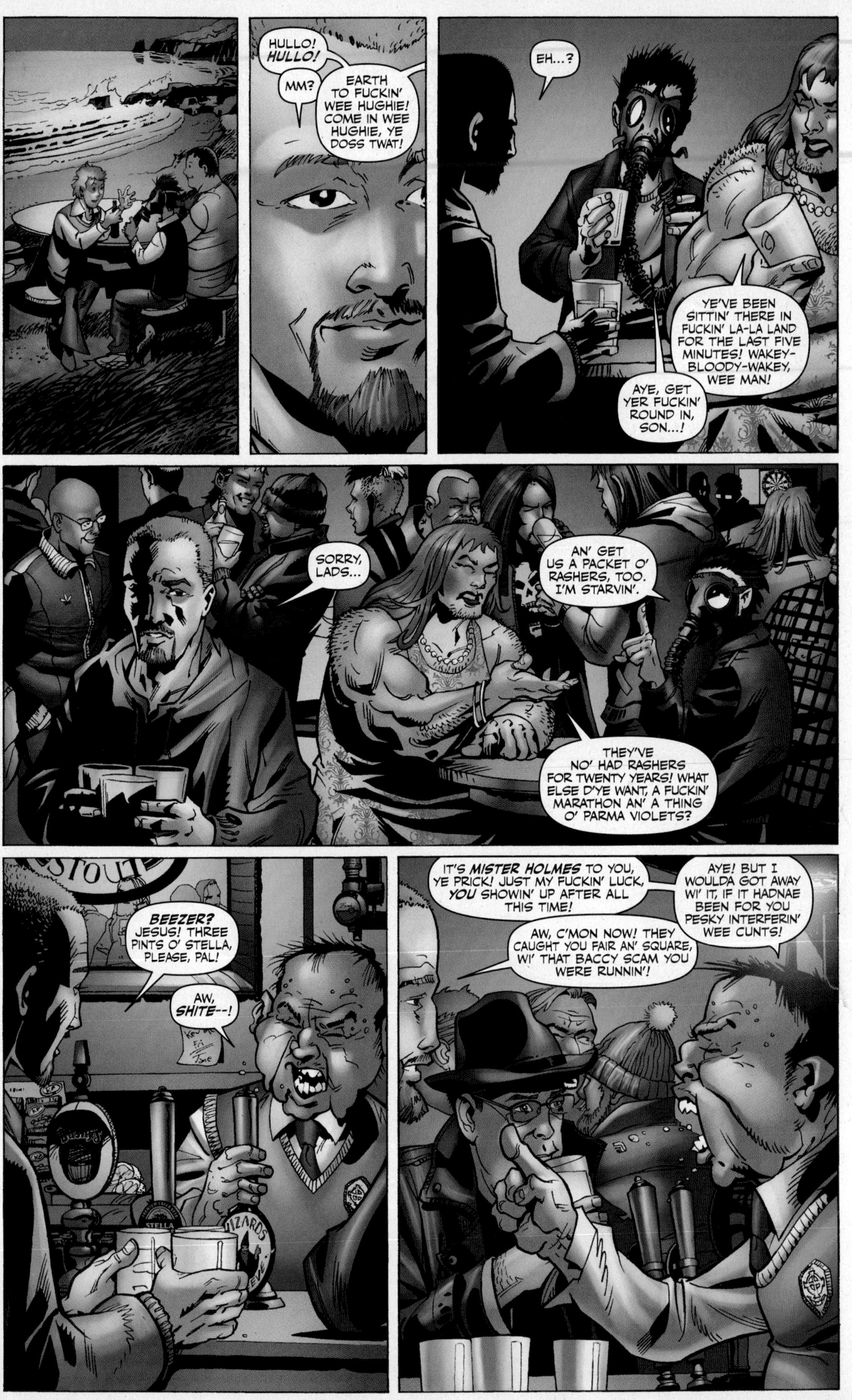

HULLO! *HULLO!*
MM?
EARTH TO FUCKIN' WEE HUGHIE! COME IN WEE HUGHIE, YE DOSS TWAT!
EH...?
YE'VE BEEN SITTIN' THERE IN FUCKIN' LA-LA LAND FOR THE LAST FIVE MINUTES! WAKEY-BLOODY-WAKEY, WEE MAN!
AYE, GET YER FUCKIN' ROUND IN, SON...!
SORRY, LADS...
AN' GET US A PACKET O' RASHERS, TOO. I'M STARVIN'.
THEY'VE NO' HAD RASHERS FOR TWENTY YEARS! WHAT ELSE D'YE WANT, A FUCKIN' MARATHON AN' A THING O' PARMA VIOLETS?
BEEZER? JESUS! THREE PINTS O' STELLA, PLEASE, PAL!
AW, *SHITE*--!
IT'S *MISTER HOLMES* TO YOU, YE PRICK! JUST MY FUCKIN' LUCK, *YOU* SHOWIN' UP AFTER ALL THIS TIME!
AW, C'MON NOW! THEY CAUGHT YOU FAIR AN' SQUARE, WI' THAT BACCY SCAM YOU WERE RUNNIN'!
AYE! BUT I WOULDA GOT AWAY WI' IT, IF IT HADNAE BEEN FOR YOU PESKY INTERFERIN' WEE CUNTS!

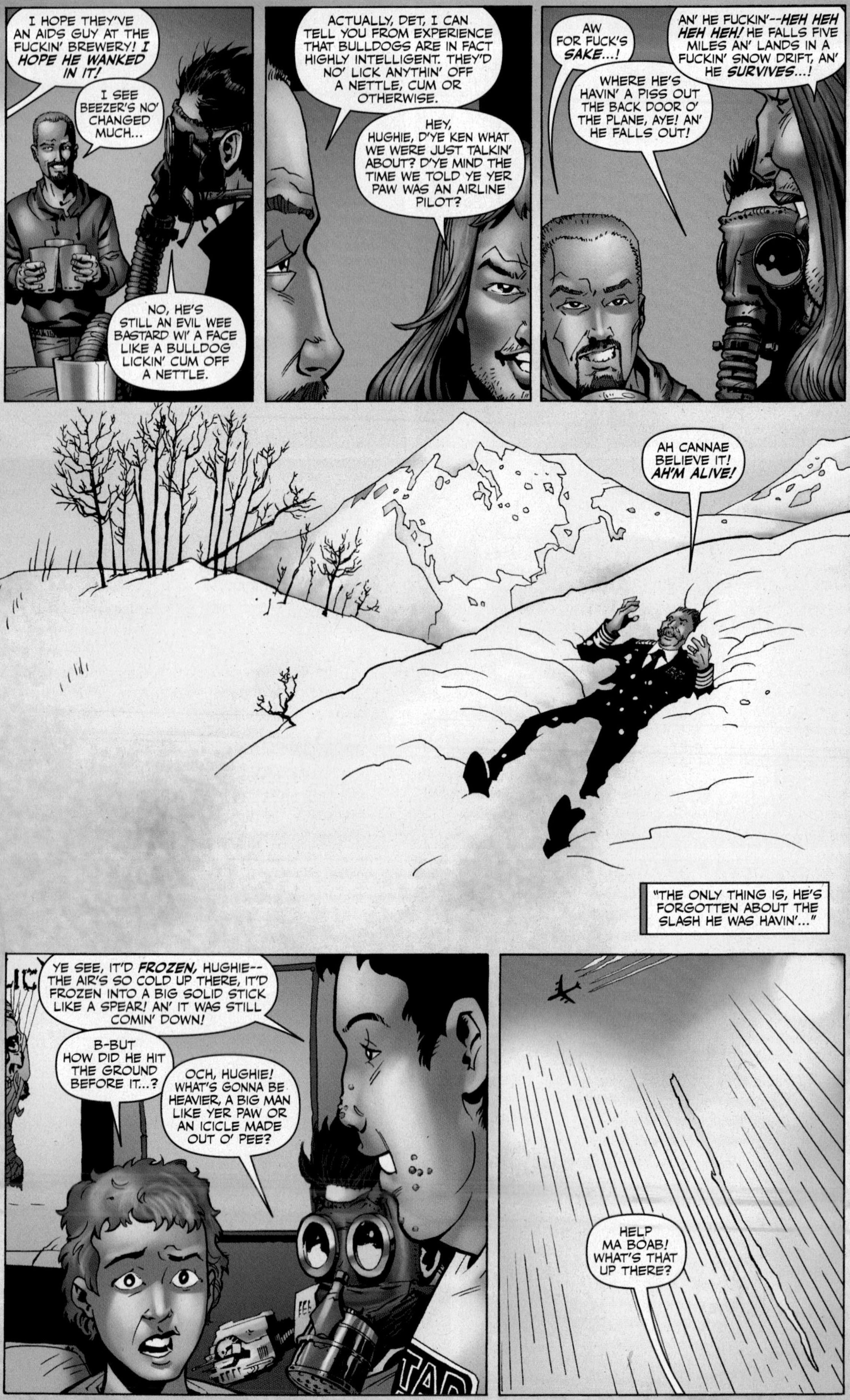

I HOPE THEY'VE AN AIDS GUY AT THE FUCKIN' BREWERY! *I HOPE HE WANKED IN IT!*
I SEE BEEZER'S NO' CHANGED MUCH...
NO, HE'S STILL AN EVIL WEE BASTARD WI' A FACE LIKE A BULLDOG LICKIN' CUM OFF A NETTLE.
ACTUALLY, DET, I CAN TELL YOU FROM EXPERIENCE THAT BULLDOGS ARE IN FACT HIGHLY INTELLIGENT. THEY'D NO' LICK ANYTHIN' OFF A NETTLE, CUM OR OTHERWISE.
HEY, HUGHIE, D'YE KEN WHAT WE WERE JUST TALKIN' ABOUT? D'YE MIND THE TIME WE TOLD YE YER PAW WAS AN AIRLINE PILOT?
AW FOR FUCK'S *SAKE*...!
WHERE HE'S HAVIN' A PISS OUT THE BACK DOOR O' THE PLANE, AYE! AN' HE FALLS OUT!
AN' HE FUCKIN'--*HEH HEH HEH HEH!* HE FALLS FIVE MILES AN' LANDS IN A FUCKIN' SNOW DRIFT, AN' HE *SURVIVES*...!
AH CANNAE BELIEVE IT! *AH'M ALIVE!*
"THE ONLY THING IS, HE'S FORGOTTEN ABOUT THE SLASH HE WAS HAVIN'..."
YE SEE, IT'D *FROZEN,* HUGHIE-- THE AIR'S SO COLD UP THERE, IT'D FROZEN INTO A BIG SOLID STICK LIKE A SPEAR! AN' IT WAS STILL COMIN' DOWN!
B-BUT HOW DID HE HIT THE GROUND BEFORE IT...?
OCH, HUGHIE! WHAT'S GONNA BE HEAVIER, A BIG MAN LIKE YER PAW OR AN ICICLE MADE OUT O' PEE?
HELP MA BOAB! WHAT'S THAT UP THERE?

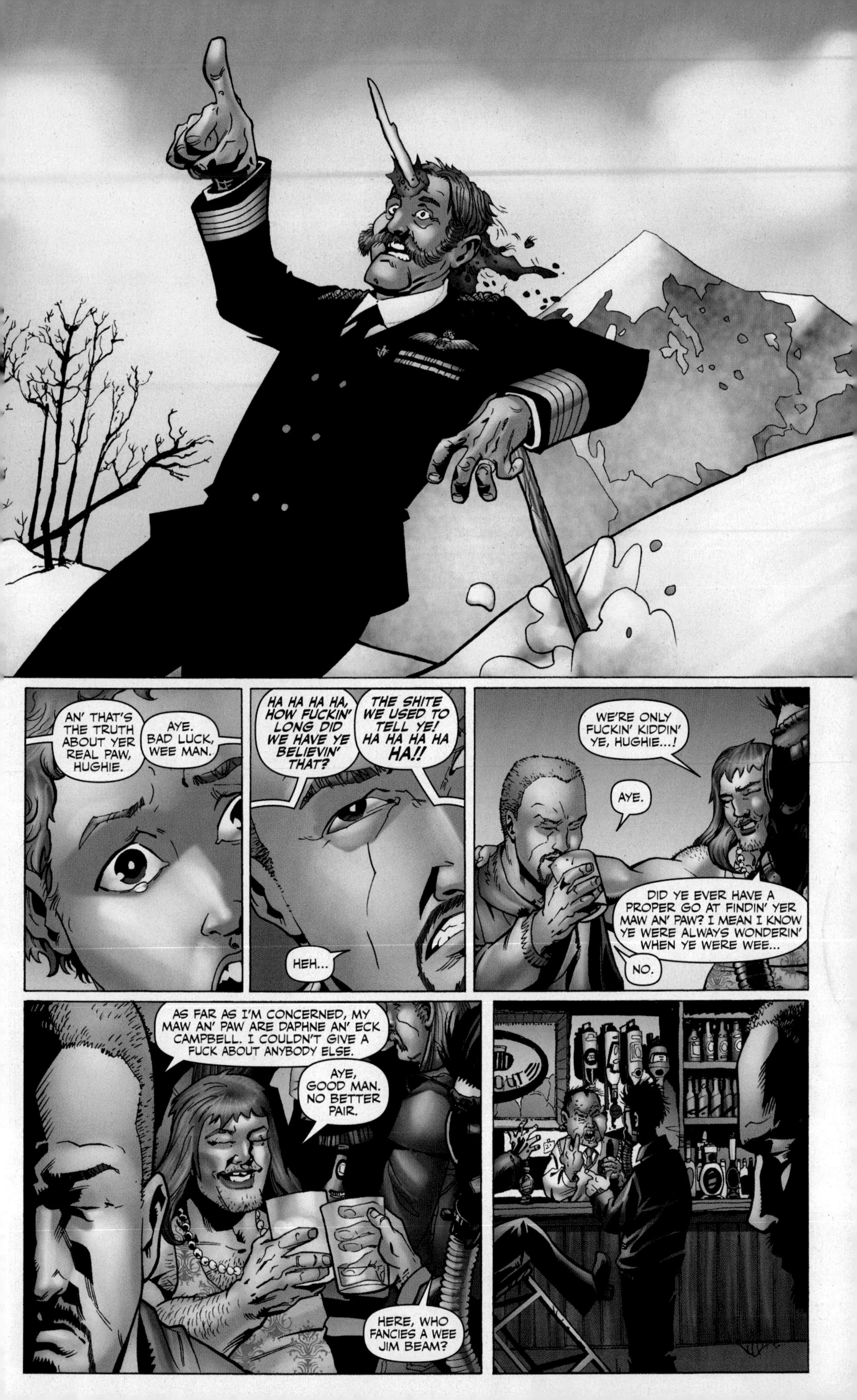
AN' THAT'S THE TRUTH ABOUT YER REAL PAW, HUGHIE.
AYE. BAD LUCK, WEE MAN.
HA HA HA HA, HOW FUCKIN' LONG DID WE HAVE YE BELIEVIN' THAT?
THE SHITE WE USED TO TELL YE! HA HA HA HA HA!!
HEH...
WE'RE ONLY FUCKIN' KIDDIN' YE, HUGHIE...!
AYE.
DID YE EVER HAVE A PROPER GO AT FINDIN' YER MAW AN' PAW? I MEAN I KNOW YE WERE ALWAYS WONDERIN' WHEN YE WERE WEE...
NO.
AS FAR AS I'M CONCERNED, MY MAW AN' PAW ARE DAPHNE AN' ECK CAMPBELL. I COULDN'T GIVE A FUCK ABOUT ANYBODY ELSE.
AYE, GOOD MAN. NO BETTER PAIR.
HERE, WHO FANCIES A WEE JIM BEAM?

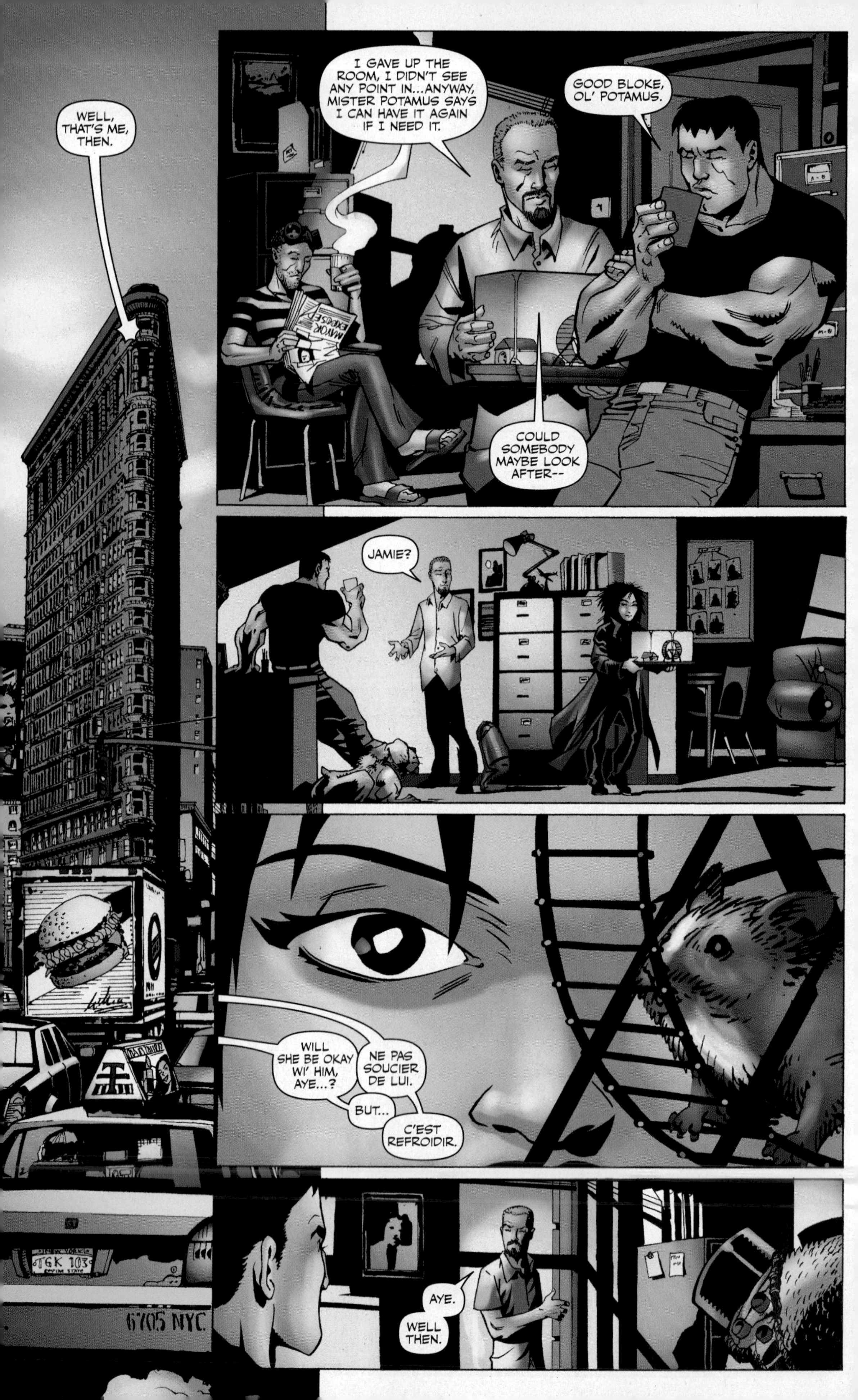
WELL, THAT'S ME, THEN.
I GAVE UP THE ROOM, I DIDN'T SEE ANY POINT IN...ANYWAY, MISTER POTAMUS SAYS I CAN HAVE IT AGAIN IF I NEED IT.
GOOD BLOKE, OL' POTAMUS.
MAYOR EXPOSE
COULD SOMEBODY MAYBE LOOK AFTER--
JAMIE?
WILL SHE BE OKAY WI' HIM, AYE...?
NE PAS SOUCIER DE LUI.
BUT...
C'EST REFROIDIR.
NEW YORK
TGK 103
6705 NYC
AYE.
WELL THEN.

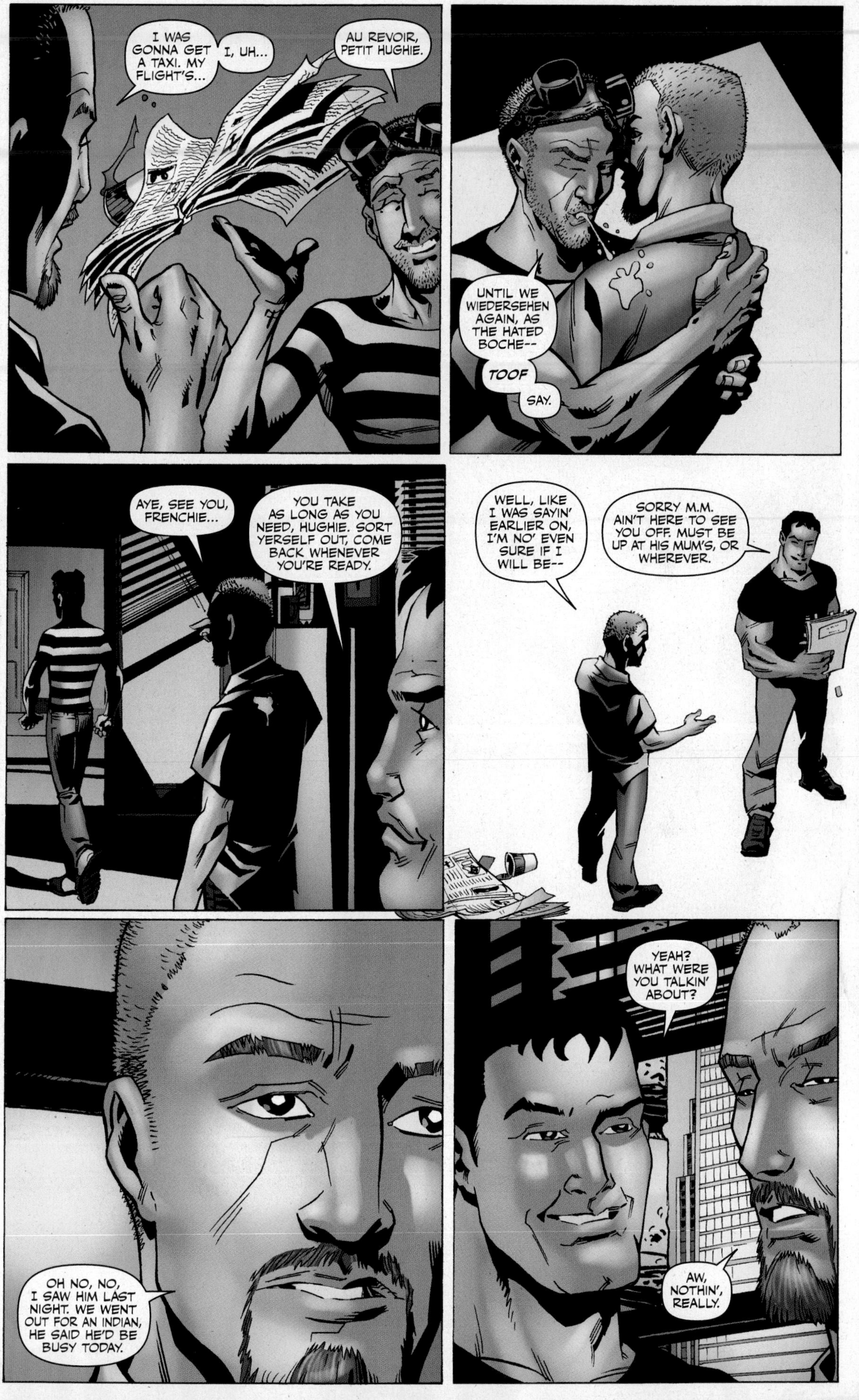
I WAS GONNA GET A TAXI. MY FLIGHT'S...
I, UH...
AU REVOIR, PETIT HUGHIE.
UNTIL WE WIEDERSEHEN AGAIN, AS THE HATED BOCHE--
TOOF
SAY.
AYE, SEE YOU, FRENCHIE...
YOU TAKE AS LONG AS YOU NEED, HUGHIE. SORT YERSELF OUT, COME BACK WHENEVER YOU'RE READY.
WELL, LIKE I WAS SAYIN' EARLIER ON, I'M NO' EVEN SURE IF I WILL BE--
SORRY M.M. AIN'T HERE TO SEE YOU OFF. MUST BE UP AT HIS MUM'S, OR WHEREVER.
OH NO, NO, I SAW HIM LAST NIGHT. WE WENT OUT FOR AN INDIAN, HE SAID HE'D BE BUSY TODAY.
YEAH? WHAT WERE YOU TALKIN' ABOUT?
AW, NOTHIN', REALLY.

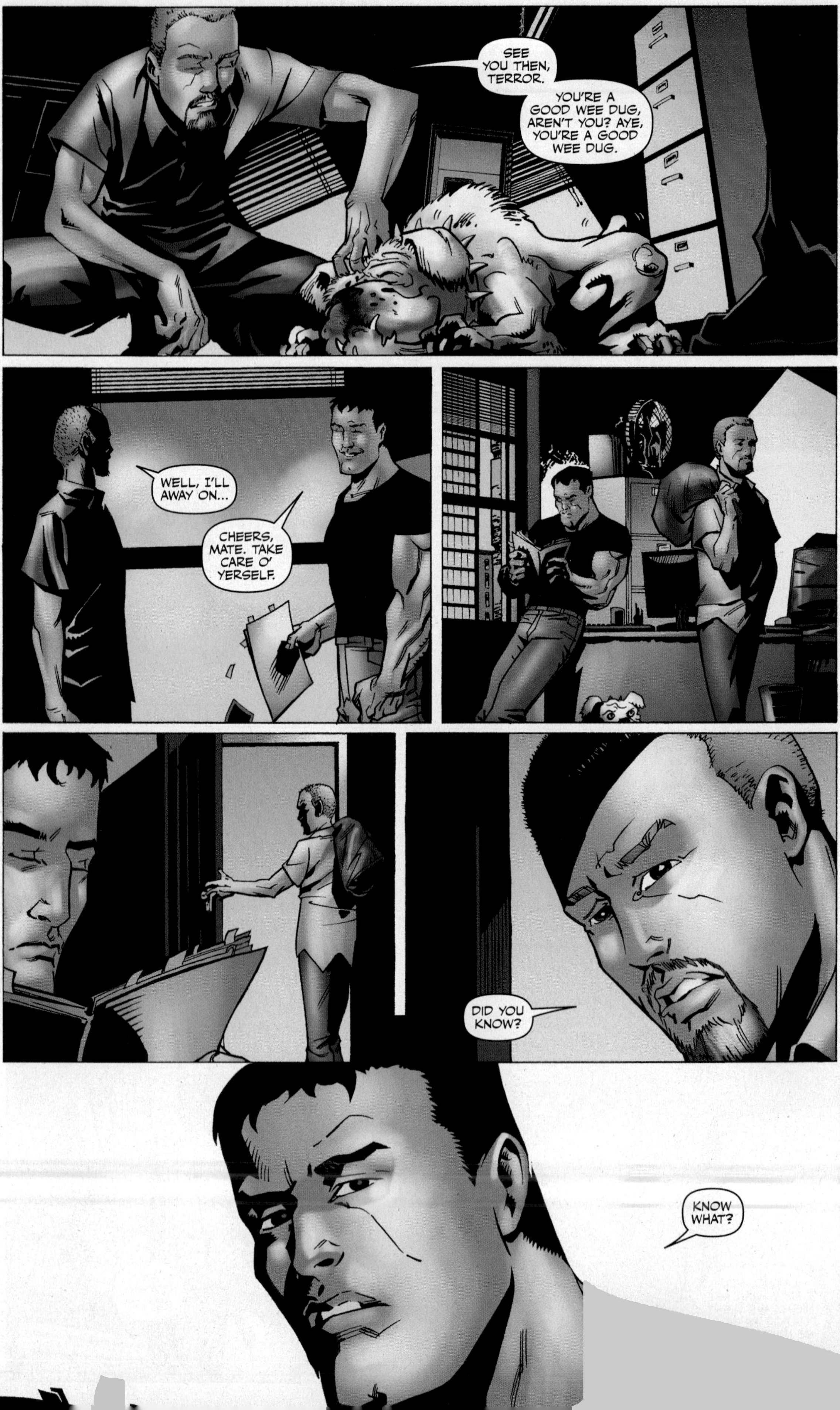
SEE YOU THEN, TERROR.
YOU'RE A GOOD WEE DUG, AREN'T YOU? AYE, YOU'RE A GOOD WEE DUG.
WELL, I'LL AWAY ON...
CHEERS, MATE. TAKE CARE O' YERSELF.
DID YOU KNOW?
KNOW WHAT?

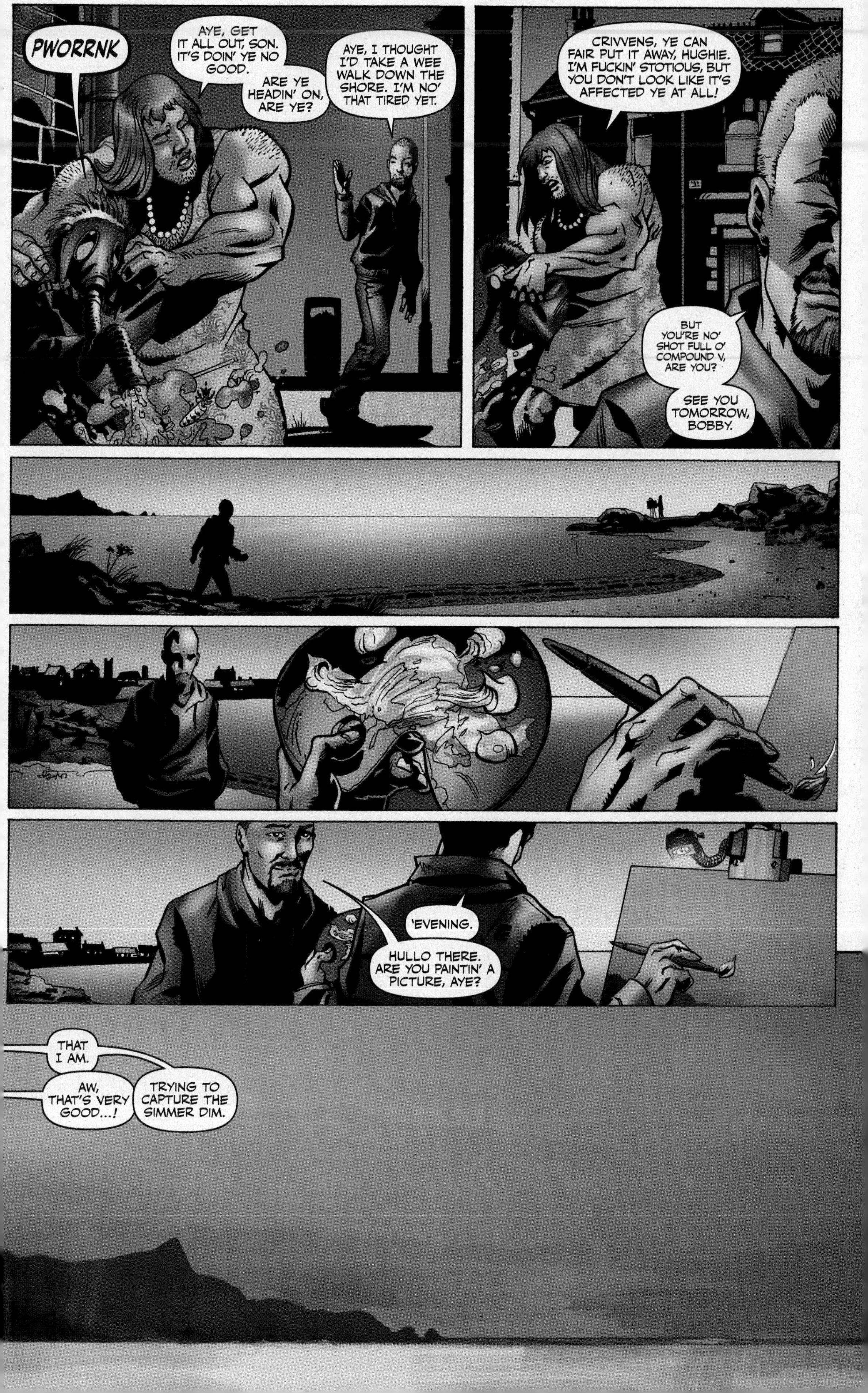
PWORRNK
AYE, GET IT ALL OUT, SON. IT'S DOIN' YE NO GOOD.
ARE YE HEADIN' ON, ARE YE?
AYE, I THOUGHT I'D TAKE A WEE WALK DOWN THE SHORE. I'M NO' THAT TIRED YET.
CRIVVENS, YE CAN FAIR PUT IT AWAY, HUGHIE. I'M FUCKIN' STOTIOUS, BUT YOU DON'T LOOK LIKE IT'S AFFECTED YE AT ALL!
BUT YOU'RE NO' SHOT FULL O' COMPOUND V, ARE YOU?
SEE YOU TOMORROW, BOBBY.
'EVENING.
HULLO THERE. ARE YOU PAINTIN' A PICTURE, AYE?
THAT I AM.
AW, THAT'S VERY GOOD...!
TRYING TO CAPTURE THE SIMMER DIM.

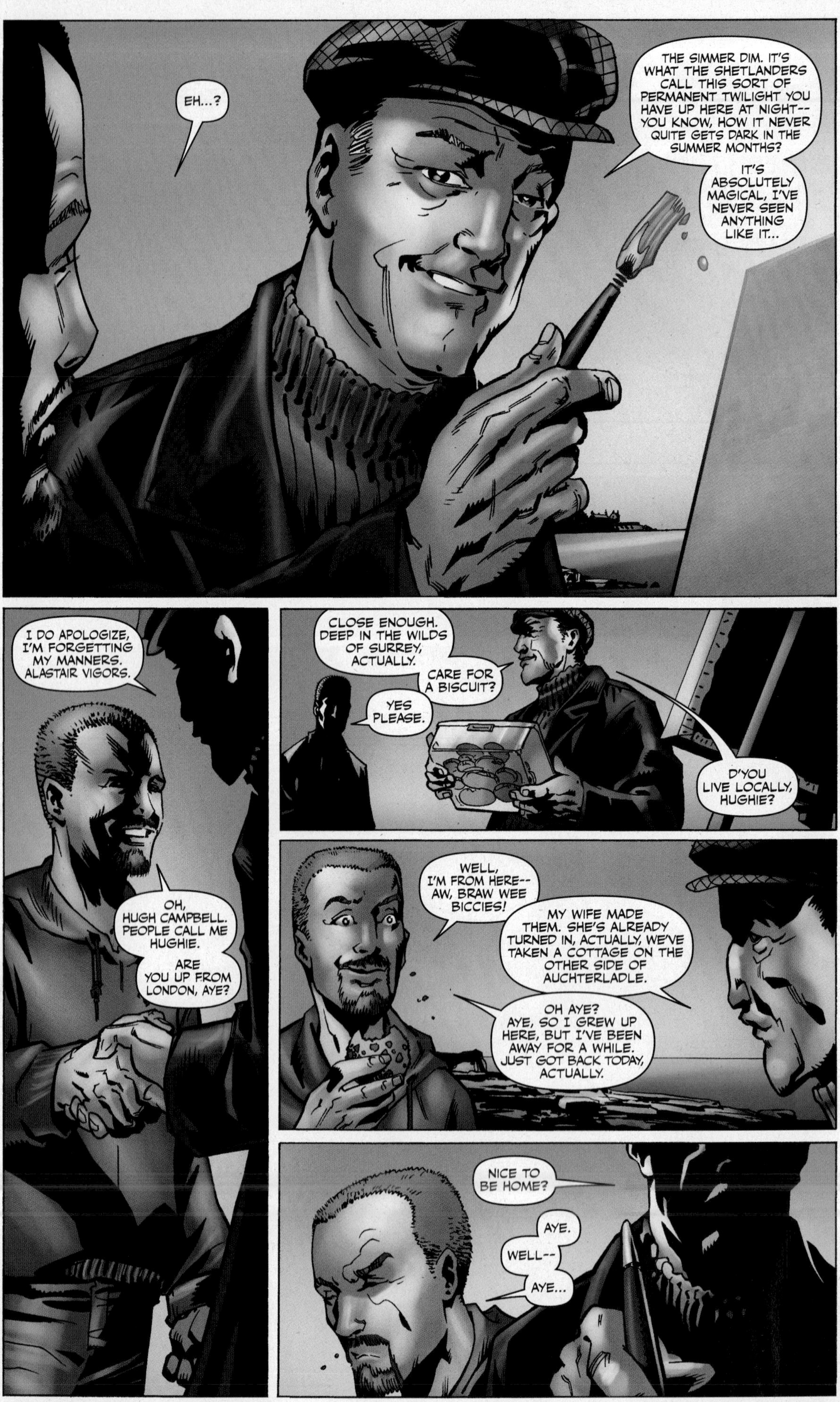
EH...?
THE SIMMER DIM. IT'S WHAT THE SHETLANDERS CALL THIS SORT OF PERMANENT TWILIGHT YOU HAVE UP HERE AT NIGHT-- YOU KNOW, HOW IT NEVER QUITE GETS DARK IN THE SUMMER MONTHS?
IT'S ABSOLUTELY MAGICAL, I'VE NEVER SEEN ANYTHING LIKE IT...
I DO APOLOGIZE, I'M FORGETTING MY MANNERS. ALASTAIR VIGORS.
OH, HUGH CAMPBELL. PEOPLE CALL ME HUGHIE.
ARE YOU UP FROM LONDON, AYE?
CLOSE ENOUGH. DEEP IN THE WILDS OF SURREY, ACTUALLY.
CARE FOR A BISCUIT?
YES PLEASE.
D'YOU LIVE LOCALLY, HUGHIE?
WELL, I'M FROM HERE-- AW, BRAW WEE BICCIES!
MY WIFE MADE THEM. SHE'S ALREADY TURNED IN, ACTUALLY, WE'VE TAKEN A COTTAGE ON THE OTHER SIDE OF AUCHTERLADLE.
OH AYE? AYE, SO I GREW UP HERE, BUT I'VE BEEN AWAY FOR A WHILE. JUST GOT BACK TODAY, ACTUALLY.
NICE TO BE HOME?
AYE.
WELL--
AYE...

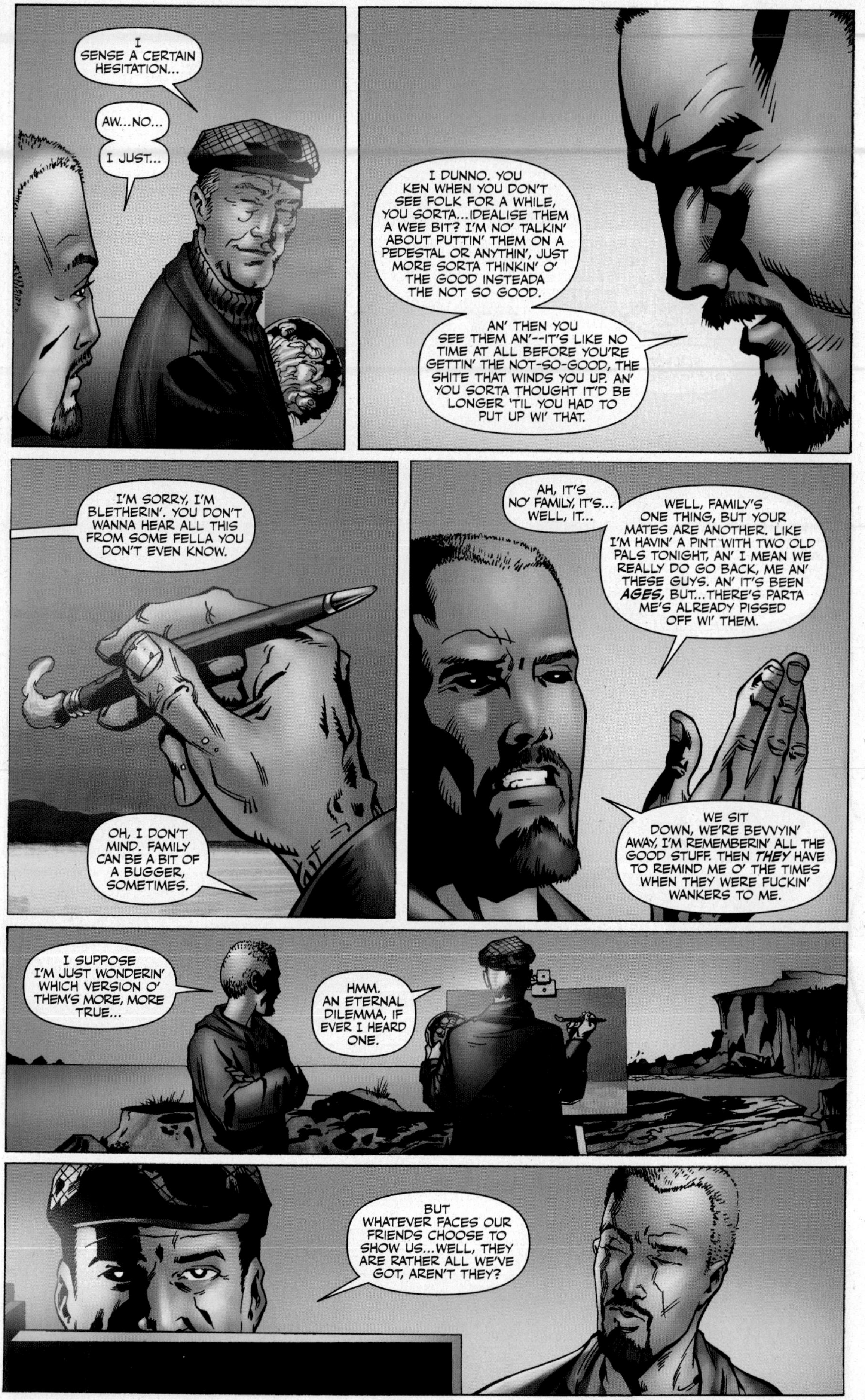

I SENSE A CERTAIN HESITATION...
AW...NO...
I JUST...
I DUNNO. YOU KEN WHEN YOU DON'T SEE FOLK FOR A WHILE, YOU SORTA...IDEALISE THEM A WEE BIT? I'M NO' TALKIN' ABOUT PUTTIN' THEM ON A PEDESTAL OR ANYTHIN', JUST MORE SORTA THINKIN' O' THE GOOD INSTEADA THE NOT SO GOOD.
AN' THEN YOU SEE THEM AN'--IT'S LIKE NO TIME AT ALL BEFORE YOU'RE GETTIN' THE NOT-SO-GOOD, THE SHITE THAT WINDS YOU UP. AN' YOU SORTA THOUGHT IT'D BE LONGER 'TIL YOU HAD TO PUT UP WI' THAT.
I'M SORRY, I'M BLETHERIN'. YOU DON'T WANNA HEAR ALL THIS FROM SOME FELLA YOU DON'T EVEN KNOW.
OH, I DON'T MIND. FAMILY CAN BE A BIT OF A BUGGER, SOMETIMES.
AH, IT'S NO' FAMILY, IT'S... WELL, IT...
WELL, FAMILY'S ONE THING, BUT YOUR MATES ARE ANOTHER. LIKE I'M HAVIN' A PINT WITH TWO OLD PALS TONIGHT, AN' I MEAN WE REALLY DO GO BACK, ME AN' THESE GUYS. AN' IT'S BEEN *AGES,* BUT...THERE'S PARTA ME'S ALREADY PISSED OFF WI' THEM.
WE SIT DOWN, WE'RE BEVVYIN' AWAY, I'M REMEMBERIN' ALL THE GOOD STUFF. THEN *THEY* HAVE TO REMIND ME O' THE TIMES WHEN THEY WERE FUCKIN' WANKERS TO ME.
I SUPPOSE I'M JUST WONDERIN' WHICH VERSION O' THEM'S MORE, MORE TRUE...
HMM. AN ETERNAL DILEMMA, IF EVER I HEARD ONE.
BUT WHATEVER FACES OUR FRIENDS CHOOSE TO SHOW US...WELL, THEY ARE RATHER ALL WE'VE GOT, AREN'T THEY?

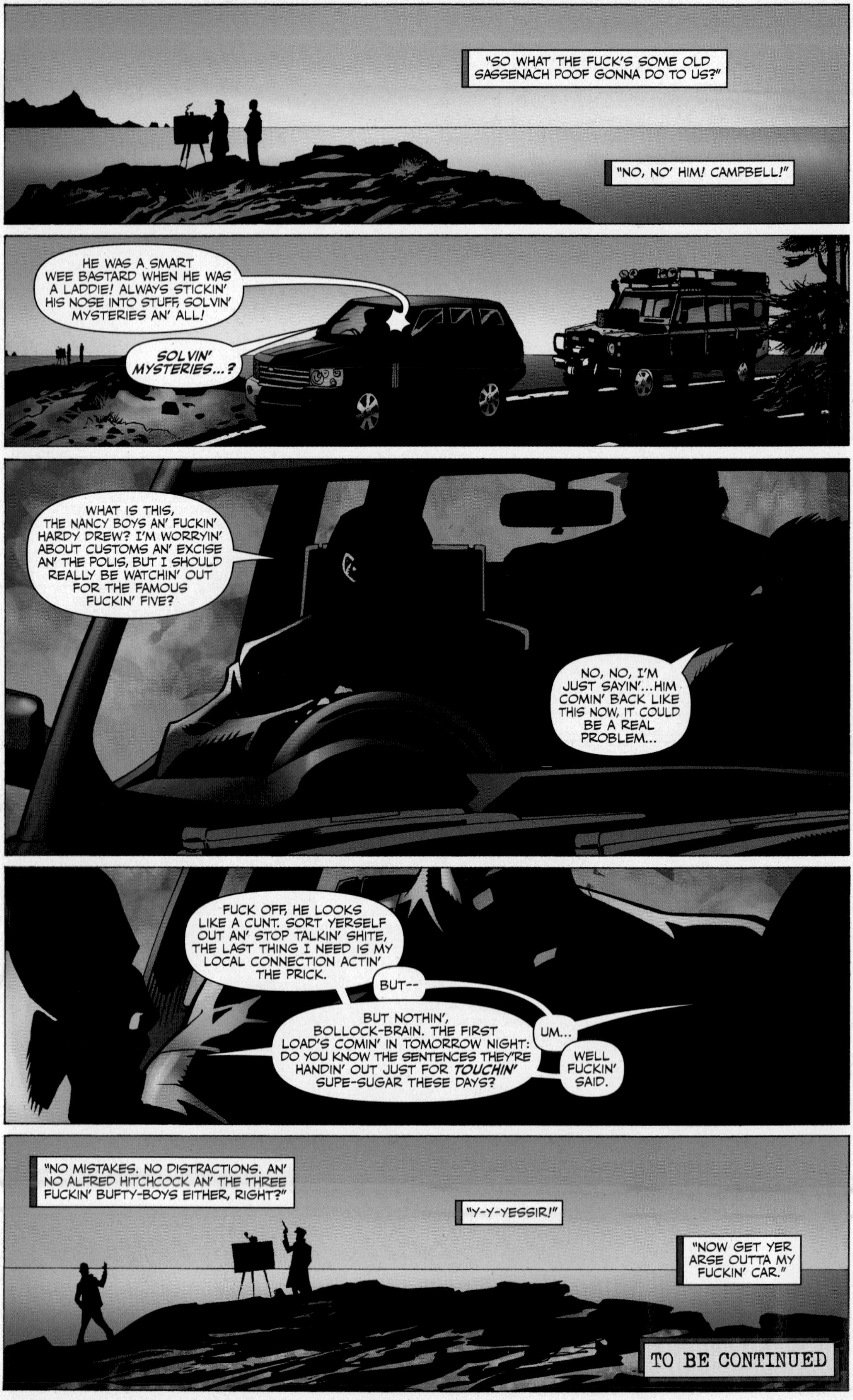
"SO WHAT THE FUCK'S SOME OLD SASSENACH POOF GONNA DO TO US?"
"NO, NO' HIM! CAMPBELL!"
HE WAS A SMART WEE BASTARD WHEN HE WAS A LADDIE! ALWAYS STICKIN' HIS NOSE INTO STUFF, SOLVIN' MYSTERIES AN' ALL!
SOLVIN' MYSTERIES...?
WHAT IS THIS, THE NANCY BOYS AN' FUCKIN' HARDY DREW? I'M WORRYIN' ABOUT CUSTOMS AN' EXCISE AN' THE POLIS, BUT I SHOULD REALLY BE WATCHIN' OUT FOR THE FAMOUS FUCKIN' FIVE?
NO, NO, I'M JUST SAYIN'...HIM COMIN' BACK LIKE THIS NOW, IT COULD BE A REAL PROBLEM...
FUCK OFF, HE LOOKS LIKE A CUNT. SORT YERSELF OUT AN' STOP TALKIN' SHITE, THE LAST THING I NEED IS MY LOCAL CONNECTION ACTIN' THE PRICK.
BUT--
BUT NOTHIN', BOLLOCK-BRAIN. THE FIRST LOAD'S COMIN' IN TOMORROW NIGHT: DO YOU KNOW THE SENTENCES THEY'RE HANDIN' OUT JUST FOR *TOUCHIN'* SUPE-SUGAR THESE DAYS?
UM...
WELL FUCKIN' SAID.
"NO MISTAKES. NO DISTRACTIONS. AN' NO ALFRED HITCHCOCK AN' THE THREE FUCKIN' BUFTY-BOYS EITHER, RIGHT?"
"Y-Y-YESSIR!"
"NOW GET YER ARSE OUTTA MY FUCKIN' CAR."
TO BE CONTINUED

two

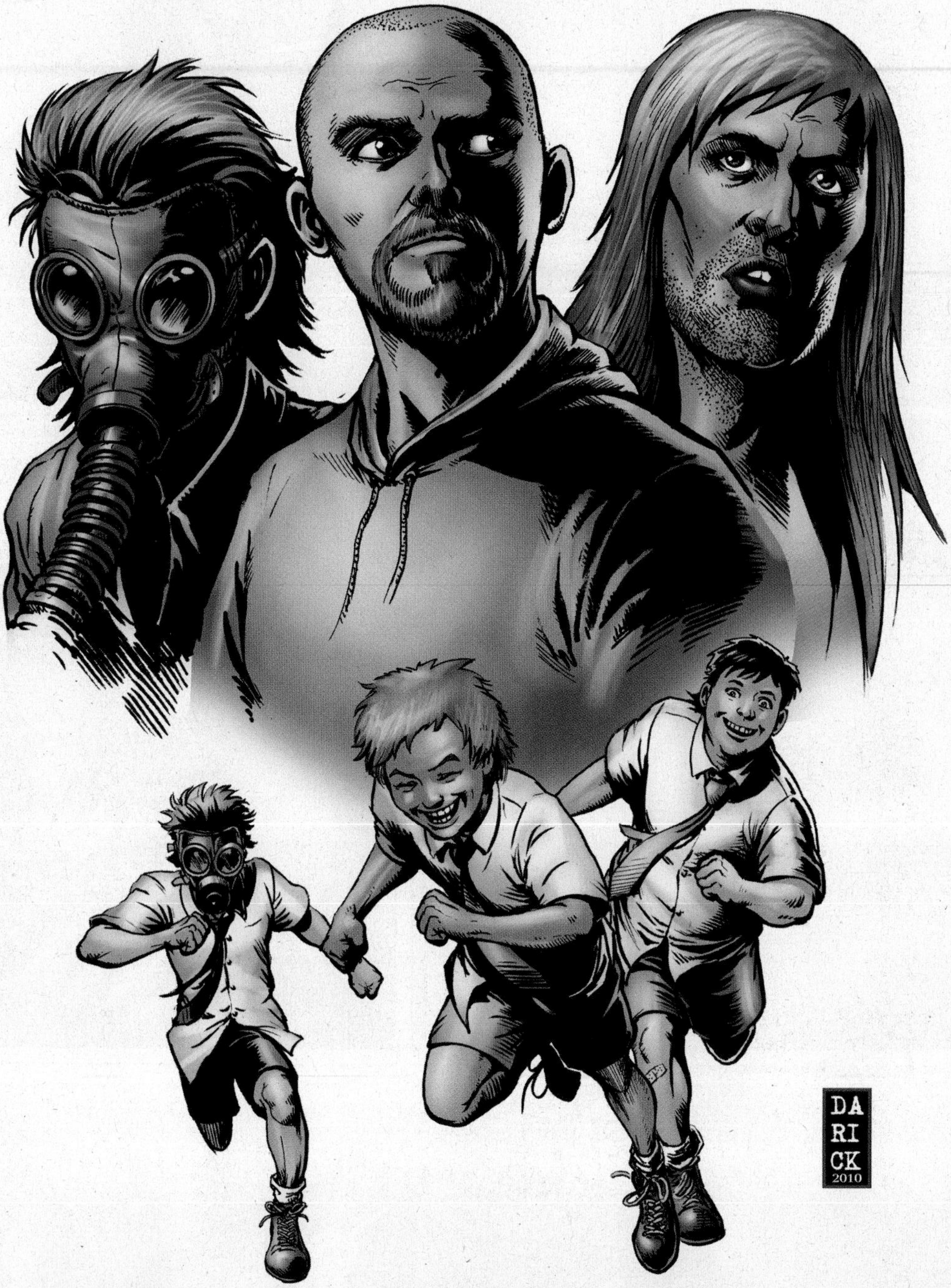
DA
RI
CK
2010

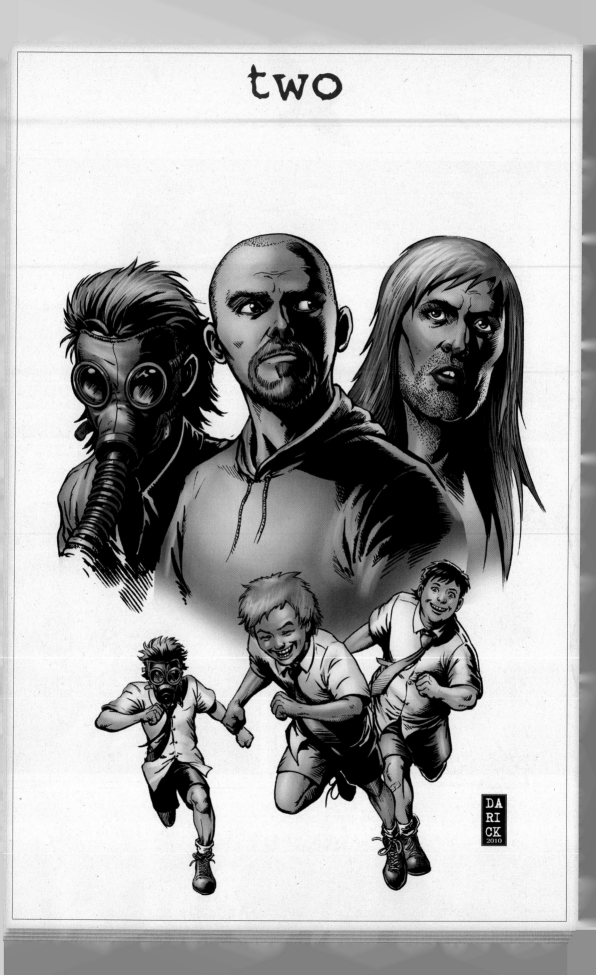

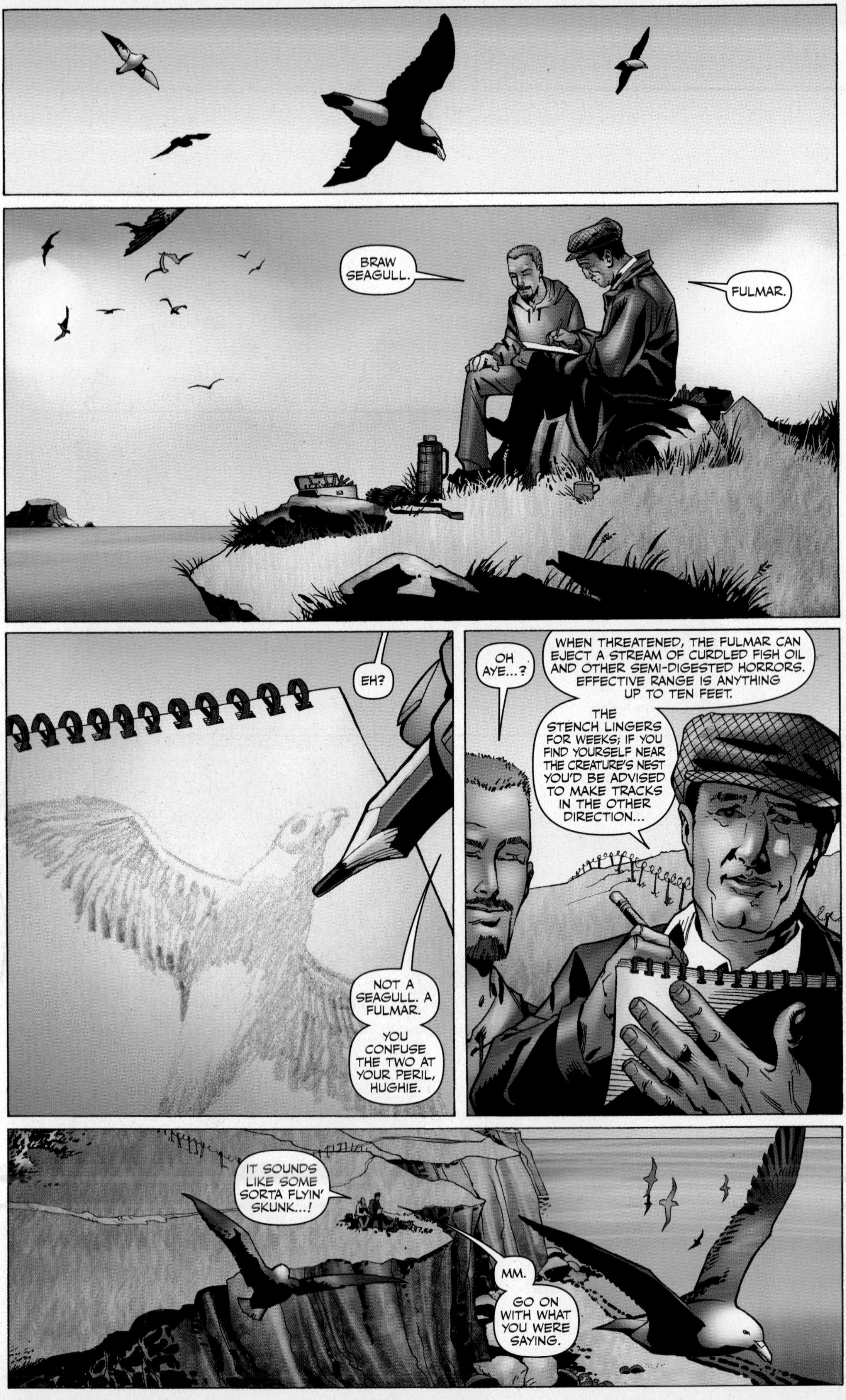
BRAW SEAGULL.
FULMAR.
EH?
NOT A SEAGULL. A FULMAR.
YOU CONFUSE THE TWO AT YOUR PERIL, HUGHIE.
OH AYE...?
WHEN THREATENED, THE FULMAR CAN EJECT A STREAM OF CURDLED FISH OIL AND OTHER SEMI-DIGESTED HORRORS. EFFECTIVE RANGE IS ANYTHING UP TO TEN FEET.
THE STENCH LINGERS FOR WEEKS; IF YOU FIND YOURSELF NEAR THE CREATURE'S NEST YOU'D BE ADVISED TO MAKE TRACKS IN THE OTHER DIRECTION...
IT SOUNDS LIKE SOME SORTA FLYIN' SKUNK...!
MM.
GO ON WITH WHAT YOU WERE SAYING.

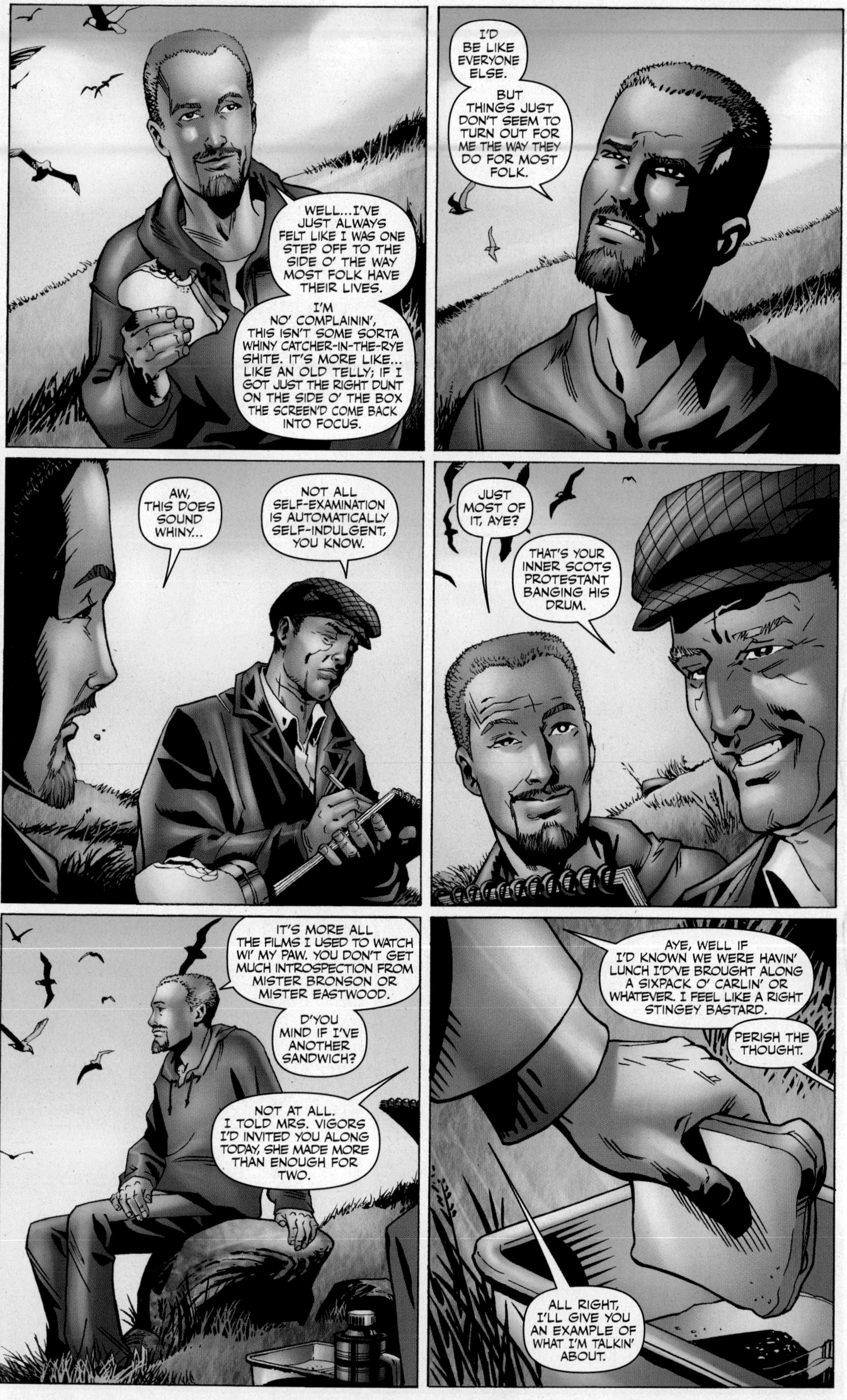
WELL...I'VE JUST ALWAYS FELT LIKE I WAS ONE STEP OFF TO THE SIDE O' THE WAY MOST FOLK HAVE THEIR LIVES.
I'M NO' COMPLAININ', THIS ISN'T SOME SORTA WHINY CATCHER-IN-THE-RYE SHITE. IT'S MORE LIKE... LIKE AN OLD TELLY; IF I GOT JUST THE RIGHT DUNT ON THE SIDE O' THE BOX THE SCREEN'D COME BACK INTO FOCUS.
I'D BE LIKE EVERYONE ELSE.
BUT THINGS JUST DON'T SEEM TO TURN OUT FOR ME THE WAY THEY DO FOR MOST FOLK.
AW, THIS DOES SOUND WHINY...
NOT ALL SELF-EXAMINATION IS AUTOMATICALLY SELF-INDULGENT, YOU KNOW.
JUST MOST OF IT, AYE?
THAT'S YOUR INNER SCOTS PROTESTANT BANGING HIS DRUM.
IT'S MORE ALL THE FILMS I USED TO WATCH WI' MY PAW. YOU DON'T GET MUCH INTROSPECTION FROM MISTER BRONSON OR MISTER EASTWOOD.
D'YOU MIND IF I'VE ANOTHER SANDWICH?
NOT AT ALL. I TOLD MRS. VIGORS I'D INVITED YOU ALONG TODAY, SHE MADE MORE THAN ENOUGH FOR TWO.
AYE, WELL IF I'D KNOWN WE WERE HAVIN' LUNCH I'D'VE BROUGHT ALONG A SIXPACK O' CARLIN' OR WHATEVER. I FEEL LIKE A RIGHT STINGEY BASTARD.
PERISH THE THOUGHT.
ALL RIGHT, I'LL GIVE YOU AN EXAMPLE OF WHAT I'M TALKIN' ABOUT.

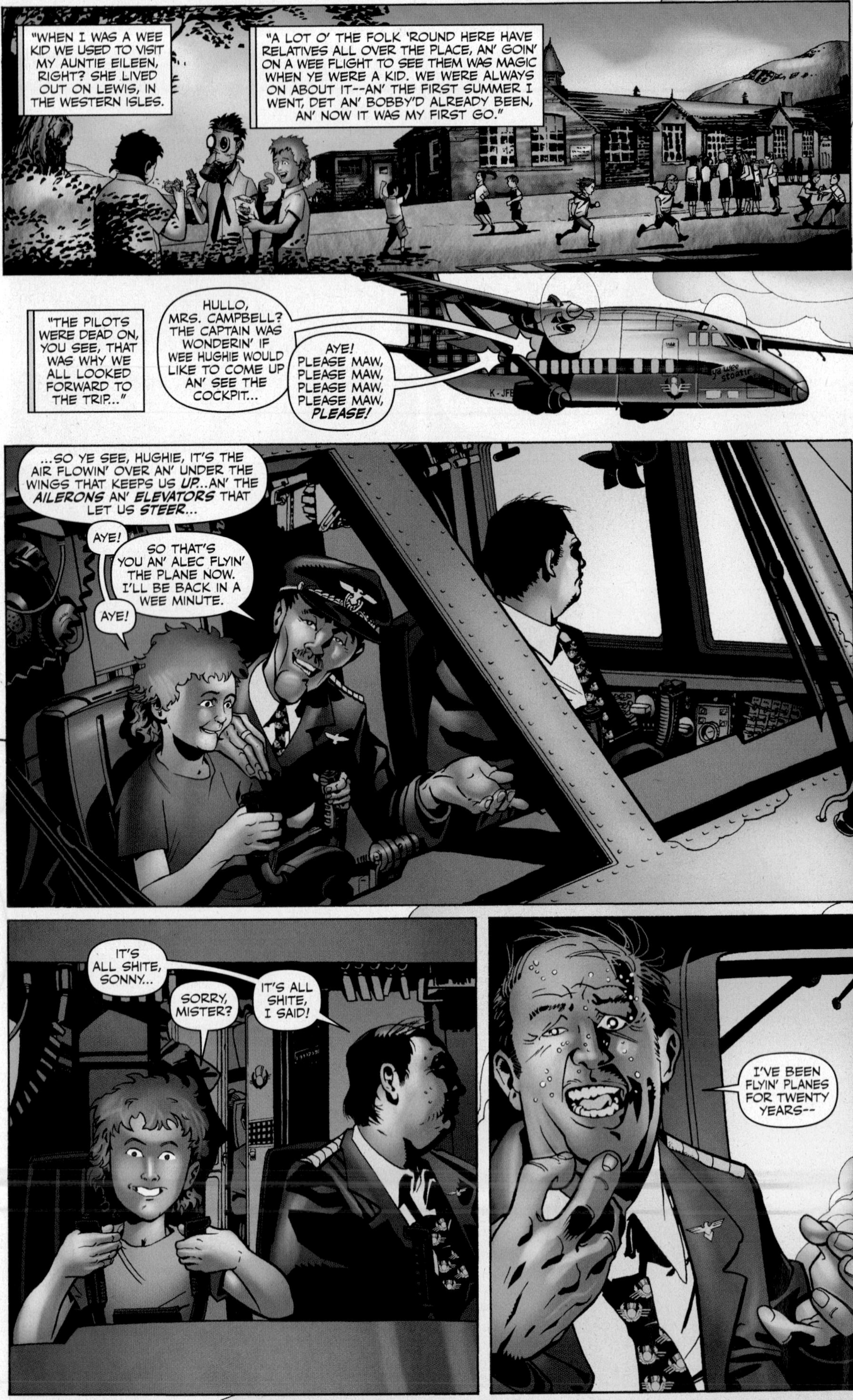
"WHEN I WAS A WEE KID WE USED TO VISIT MY AUNTIE EILEEN, RIGHT? SHE LIVED OUT ON LEWIS, IN THE WESTERN ISLES.
"A LOT O' THE FOLK 'ROUND HERE HAVE RELATIVES ALL OVER THE PLACE, AN' GOIN' ON A WEE FLIGHT TO SEE THEM WAS MAGIC WHEN YE WERE A KID. WE WERE ALWAYS ON ABOUT IT--AN' THE FIRST SUMMER I WENT, DET AN' BOBBY'D ALREADY BEEN, AN' NOW IT WAS MY FIRST GO."
"THE PILOTS WERE DEAD ON, YOU SEE, THAT WAS WHY WE ALL LOOKED FORWARD TO THE TRIP..."
HULLO, MRS. CAMPBELL? THE CAPTAIN WAS WONDERIN' IF WEE HUGHIE WOULD LIKE TO COME UP AN' SEE THE COCKPIT...
AYE! PLEASE MAW, PLEASE MAW, PLEASE MAW, PLEASE MAW, PLEASE!
...SO YE SEE, HUGHIE, IT'S THE AIR FLOWIN' OVER AN' UNDER THE WINGS THAT KEEPS US UP...AN' THE AILERONS AN' ELEVATORS THAT LET US STEER...
AYE!
SO THAT'S YOU AN' ALEC FLYIN' THE PLANE NOW. I'LL BE BACK IN A WEE MINUTE.
AYE!
IT'S ALL SHITE, SONNY...
SORRY, MISTER?
IT'S ALL SHITE, I SAID!
I'VE BEEN FLYIN' PLANES FOR TWENTY YEARS--

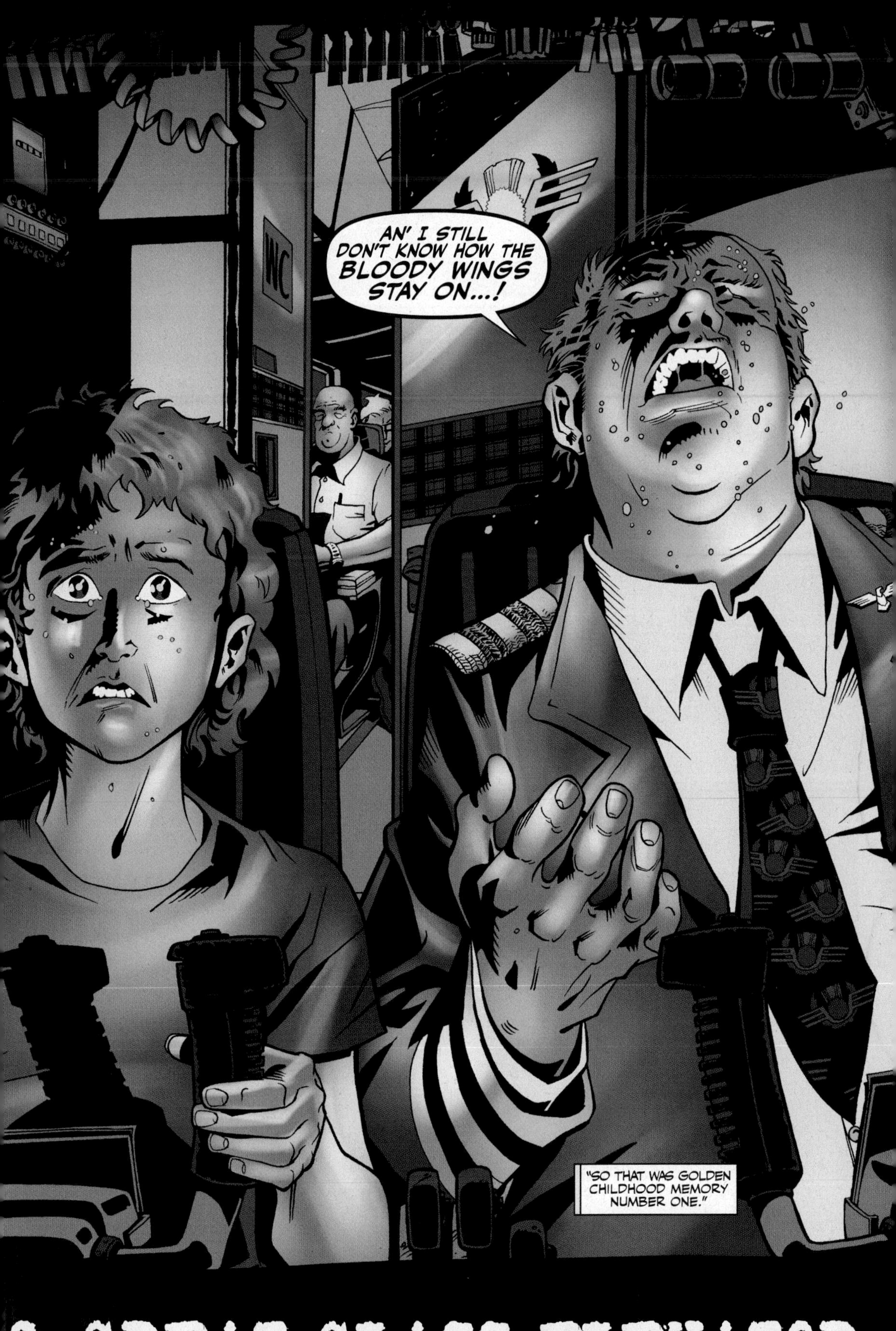
AN' I STILL DON'T KNOW HOW THE BLOODY WINGS STAY ON...!
WC
"SO THAT WAS GOLDEN CHILDHOOD MEMORY NUMBER ONE."

2: GREAT GLASS ELEVATOR

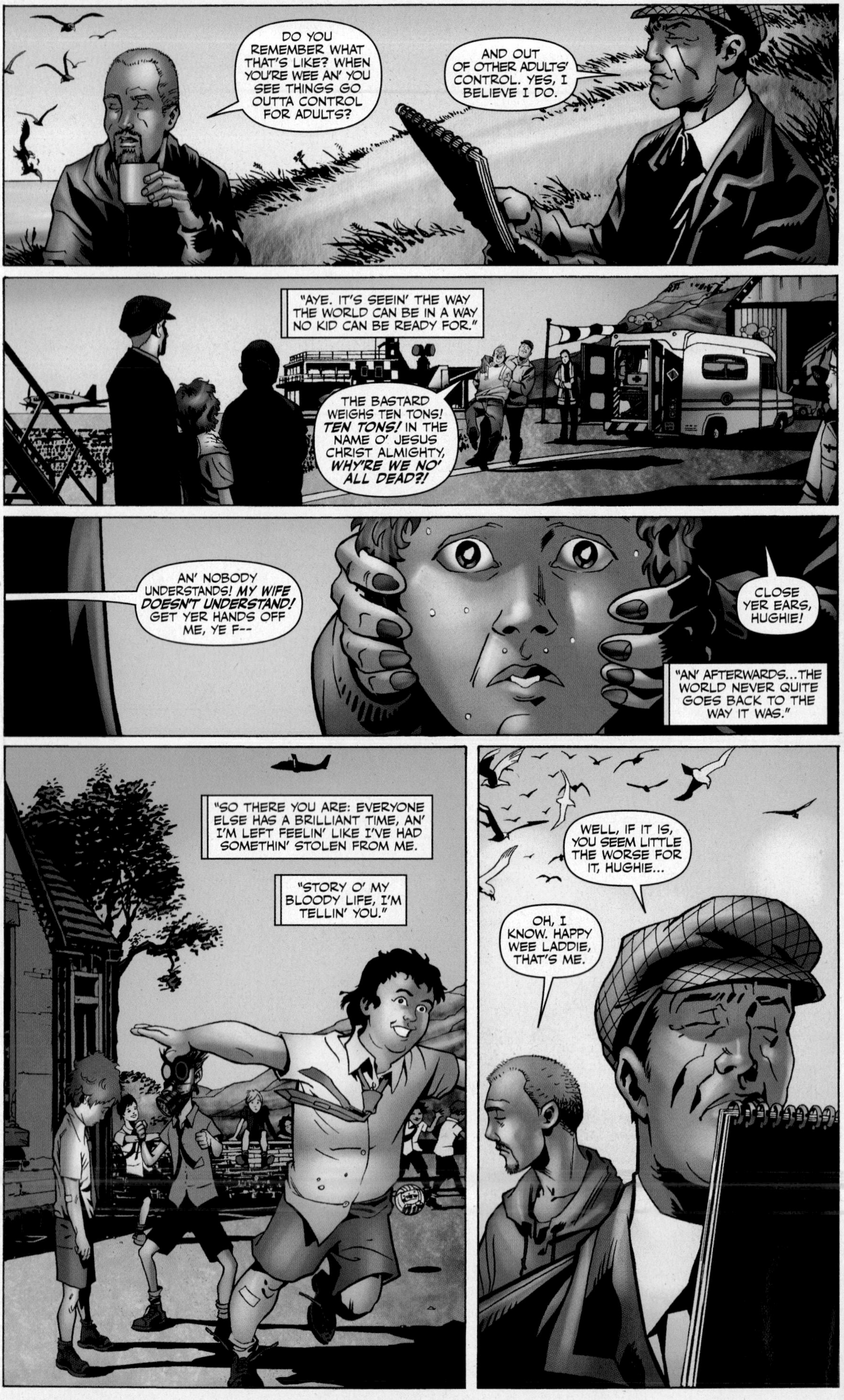
DO YOU REMEMBER WHAT THAT'S LIKE? WHEN YOU'RE WEE AN' YOU SEE THINGS GO OUTTA CONTROL FOR ADULTS?
AND OUT OF OTHER ADULTS' CONTROL. YES, I BELIEVE I DO.
"AYE. IT'S SEEIN' THE WAY THE WORLD CAN BE IN A WAY NO KID CAN BE READY FOR."
THE BASTARD WEIGHS TEN TONS! *TEN TONS!* IN THE NAME O' JESUS CHRIST ALMIGHTY, *WHY'RE WE NO' ALL DEAD?!*
AN' NOBODY UNDERSTANDS! *MY WIFE DOESN'T UNDERSTAND!* GET YER HANDS OFF ME, YE F--
CLOSE YER EARS, HUGHIE!
"AN' AFTERWARDS...THE WORLD NEVER QUITE GOES BACK TO THE WAY IT WAS."
"SO THERE YOU ARE: EVERYONE ELSE HAS A BRILLIANT TIME, AN' I'M LEFT FEELIN' LIKE I'VE HAD SOMETHIN' STOLEN FROM ME.
"STORY O' MY BLOODY LIFE, I'M TELLIN' YOU."
WELL, IF IT IS, YOU SEEM LITTLE THE WORSE FOR IT, HUGHIE...
OH, I KNOW. HAPPY WEE LADDIE, THAT'S ME.

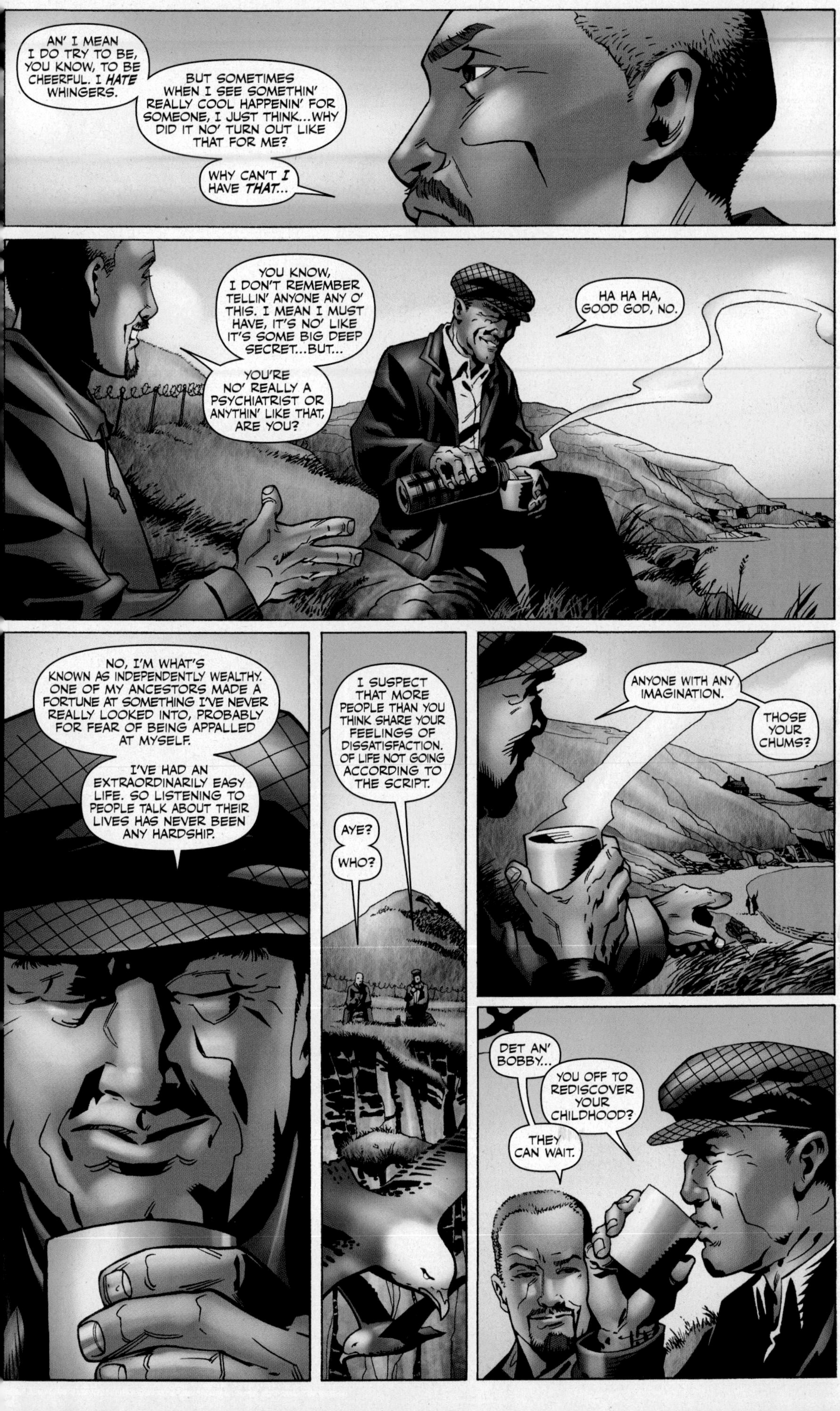

AN' I MEAN I DO TRY TO BE, YOU KNOW, TO BE CHEERFUL. I HATE WHINGERS.
BUT SOMETIMES WHEN I SEE SOMETHIN' REALLY COOL HAPPENIN' FOR SOMEONE, I JUST THINK...WHY DID IT NO' TURN OUT LIKE THAT FOR ME?
WHY CAN'T I HAVE THAT...
YOU KNOW, I DON'T REMEMBER TELLIN' ANYONE ANY O' THIS. I MEAN I MUST HAVE, IT'S NO' LIKE IT'S SOME BIG DEEP SECRET...BUT...
YOU'RE NO' REALLY A PSYCHIATRIST OR ANYTHIN' LIKE THAT, ARE YOU?
HA HA HA, GOOD GOD, NO.
NO, I'M WHAT'S KNOWN AS INDEPENDENTLY WEALTHY. ONE OF MY ANCESTORS MADE A FORTUNE AT SOMETHING I'VE NEVER REALLY LOOKED INTO, PROBABLY FOR FEAR OF BEING APPALLED AT MYSELF.
I'VE HAD AN EXTRAORDINARILY EASY LIFE. SO LISTENING TO PEOPLE TALK ABOUT THEIR LIVES HAS NEVER BEEN ANY HARDSHIP.
I SUSPECT THAT MORE PEOPLE THAN YOU THINK SHARE YOUR FEELINGS OF DISSATISFACTION. OF LIFE NOT GOING ACCORDING TO THE SCRIPT.
AYE?
WHO?
ANYONE WITH ANY IMAGINATION.
THOSE YOUR CHUMS?
DET AN' BOBBY...
YOU OFF TO REDISCOVER YOUR CHILDHOOD?
THEY CAN WAIT.

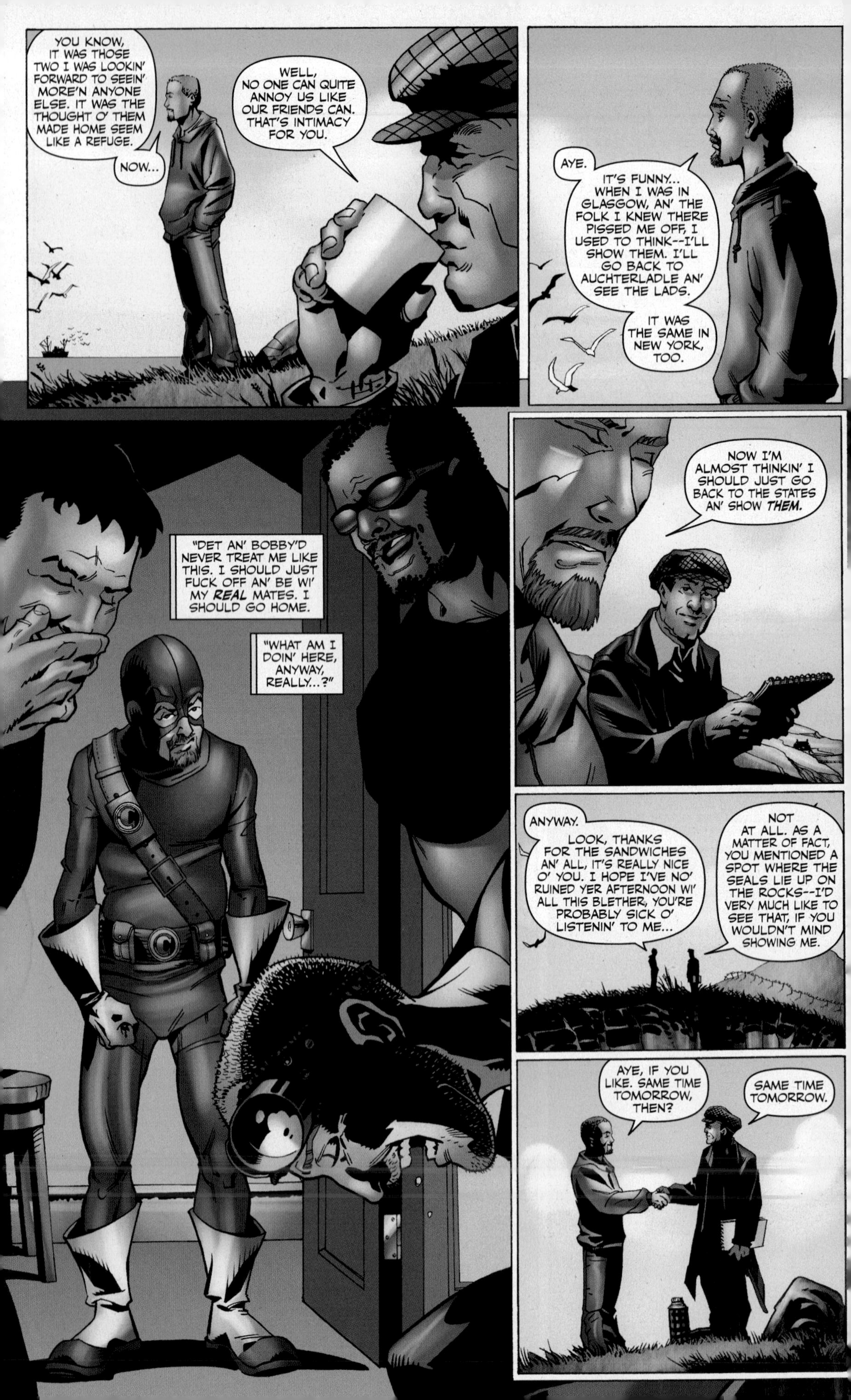
YOU KNOW, IT WAS THOSE TWO I WAS LOOKIN' FORWARD TO SEEIN' MORE'N ANYONE ELSE. IT WAS THE THOUGHT O' THEM MADE HOME SEEM LIKE A REFUGE.
NOW...
WELL, NO ONE CAN QUITE ANNOY US LIKE OUR FRIENDS CAN. THAT'S INTIMACY FOR YOU.
AYE.
IT'S FUNNY... WHEN I WAS IN GLASGOW, AN' THE FOLK I KNEW THERE PISSED ME OFF, I USED TO THINK--I'LL SHOW THEM. I'LL GO BACK TO AUCHTERLADLE AN' SEE THE LADS.
IT WAS THE SAME IN NEW YORK, TOO.
"DET AN' BOBBY'D NEVER TREAT ME LIKE THIS. I SHOULD JUST FUCK OFF AN' BE WI' MY *REAL* MATES. I SHOULD GO HOME.
"WHAT AM I DOIN' HERE, ANYWAY, REALLY...?"
NOW I'M ALMOST THINKIN' I SHOULD JUST GO BACK TO THE STATES AN' SHOW *THEM.*
ANYWAY.
LOOK, THANKS FOR THE SANDWICHES AN' ALL, IT'S REALLY NICE O' YOU. I HOPE I'VE NO' RUINED YER AFTERNOON WI' ALL THIS BLETHER, YOU'RE PROBABLY SICK O' LISTENIN' TO ME...
NOT AT ALL. AS A MATTER OF FACT, YOU MENTIONED A SPOT WHERE THE SEALS LIE UP ON THE ROCKS--I'D VERY MUCH LIKE TO SEE THAT, IF YOU WOULDN'T MIND SHOWING ME.
AYE, IF YOU LIKE. SAME TIME TOMORROW, THEN?
SAME TIME TOMORROW.

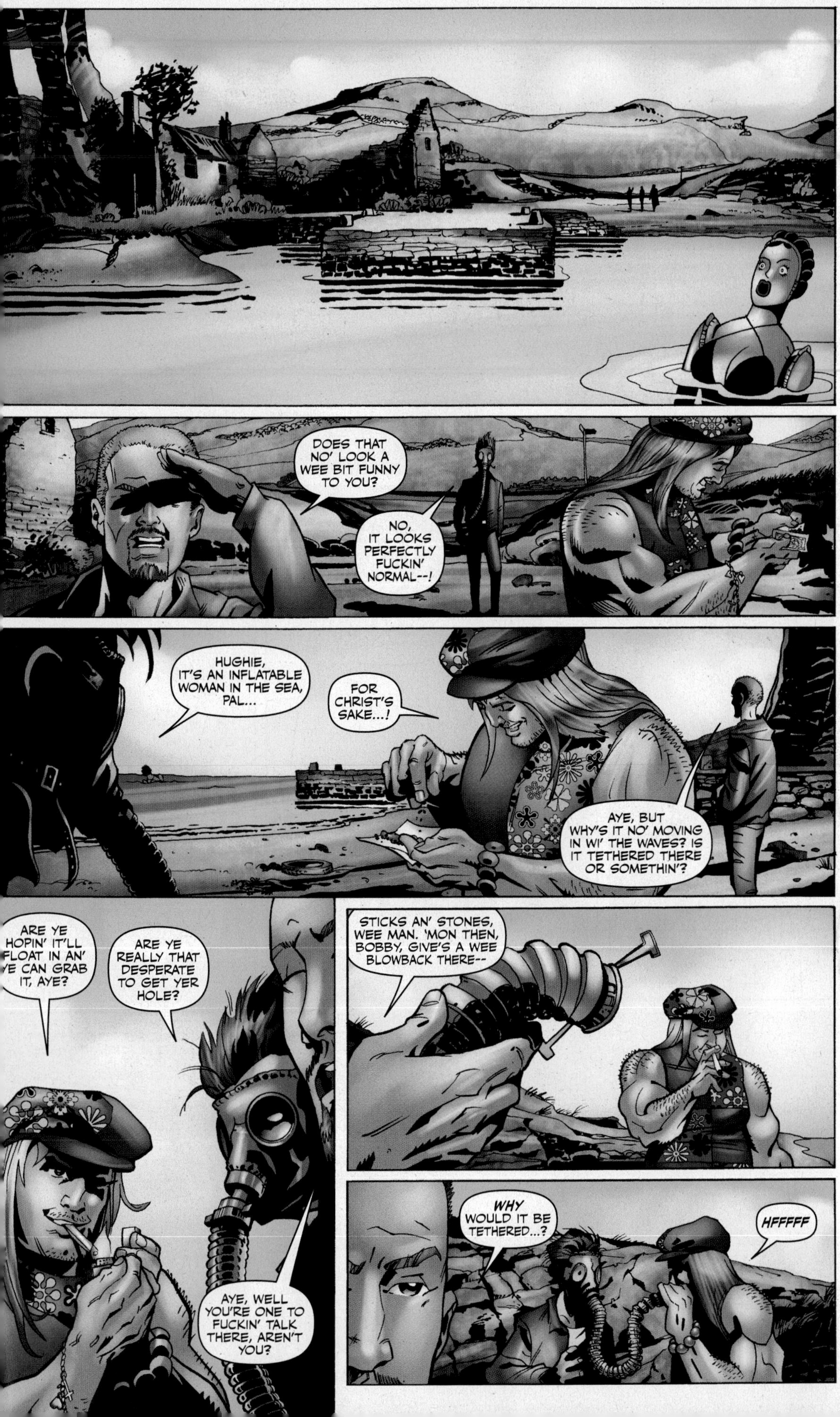

DOES THAT NO' LOOK A WEE BIT FUNNY TO YOU?
NO, IT LOOKS PERFECTLY FUCKIN' NORMAL--!
HUGHIE, IT'S AN INFLATABLE WOMAN IN THE SEA, PAL...
FOR CHRIST'S SAKE...!
AYE, BUT WHY'S IT NO' MOVING IN WI' THE WAVES? IS IT TETHERED THERE OR SOMETHIN'?
ARE YE HOPIN' IT'LL FLOAT IN AN' YE CAN GRAB IT, AYE?
ARE YE REALLY THAT DESPERATE TO GET YER HOLE?
AYE, WELL YOU'RE ONE TO FUCKIN' TALK THERE, AREN'T YOU?
STICKS AN' STONES, WEE MAN. 'MON THEN, BOBBY, GIVE'S A WEE BLOWBACK THERE--
WHY WOULD IT BE TETHERED...?
HFFFFF

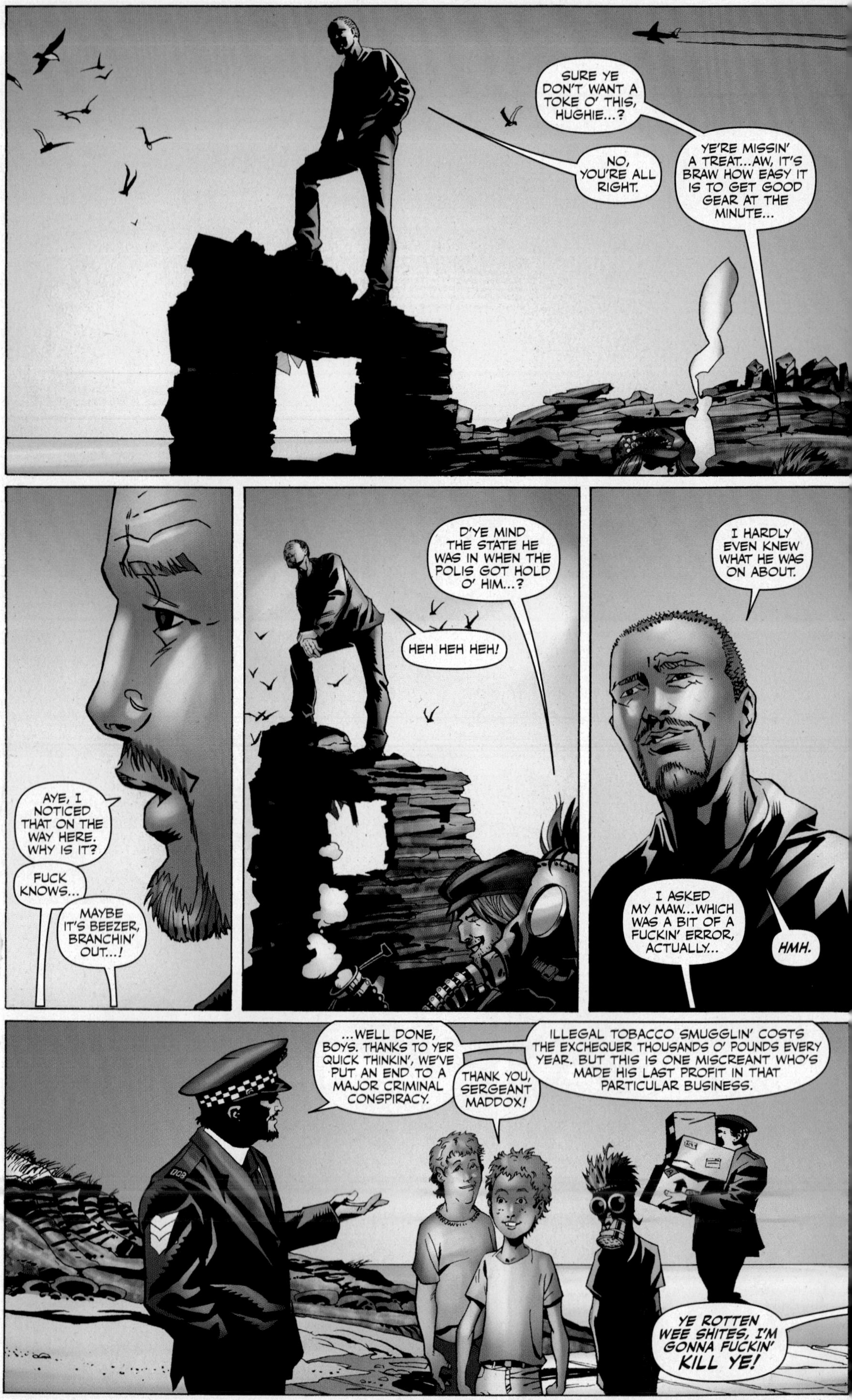
SURE YE DON'T WANT A TOKE O' THIS, HUGHIE...?
NO, YOU'RE ALL RIGHT.
YE'RE MISSIN' A TREAT...AW, IT'S BRAW HOW EASY IT IS TO GET GOOD GEAR AT THE MINUTE...
AYE, I NOTICED THAT ON THE WAY HERE. WHY IS IT?
FUCK KNOWS...
MAYBE IT'S BEEZER, BRANCHIN' OUT...!
D'YE MIND THE STATE HE WAS IN WHEN THE POLIS GOT HOLD O' HIM...?
HEH HEH HEH!
I HARDLY EVEN KNEW WHAT HE WAS ON ABOUT.
I ASKED MY MAW...WHICH WAS A BIT OF A FUCKIN' ERROR, ACTUALLY...
HMH.
...WELL DONE, BOYS. THANKS TO YER QUICK THINKIN', WE'VE PUT AN END TO A MAJOR CRIMINAL CONSPIRACY.
ILLEGAL TOBACCO SMUGGLIN' COSTS THE EXCHEQUER THOUSANDS O' POUNDS EVERY YEAR. BUT THIS IS ONE MISCREANT WHO'S MADE HIS LAST PROFIT IN THAT PARTICULAR BUSINESS.
THANK YOU, SERGEANT MADDOX!
YE ROTTEN WEE SHITES, I'M GONNA FUCKIN' KILL YE!

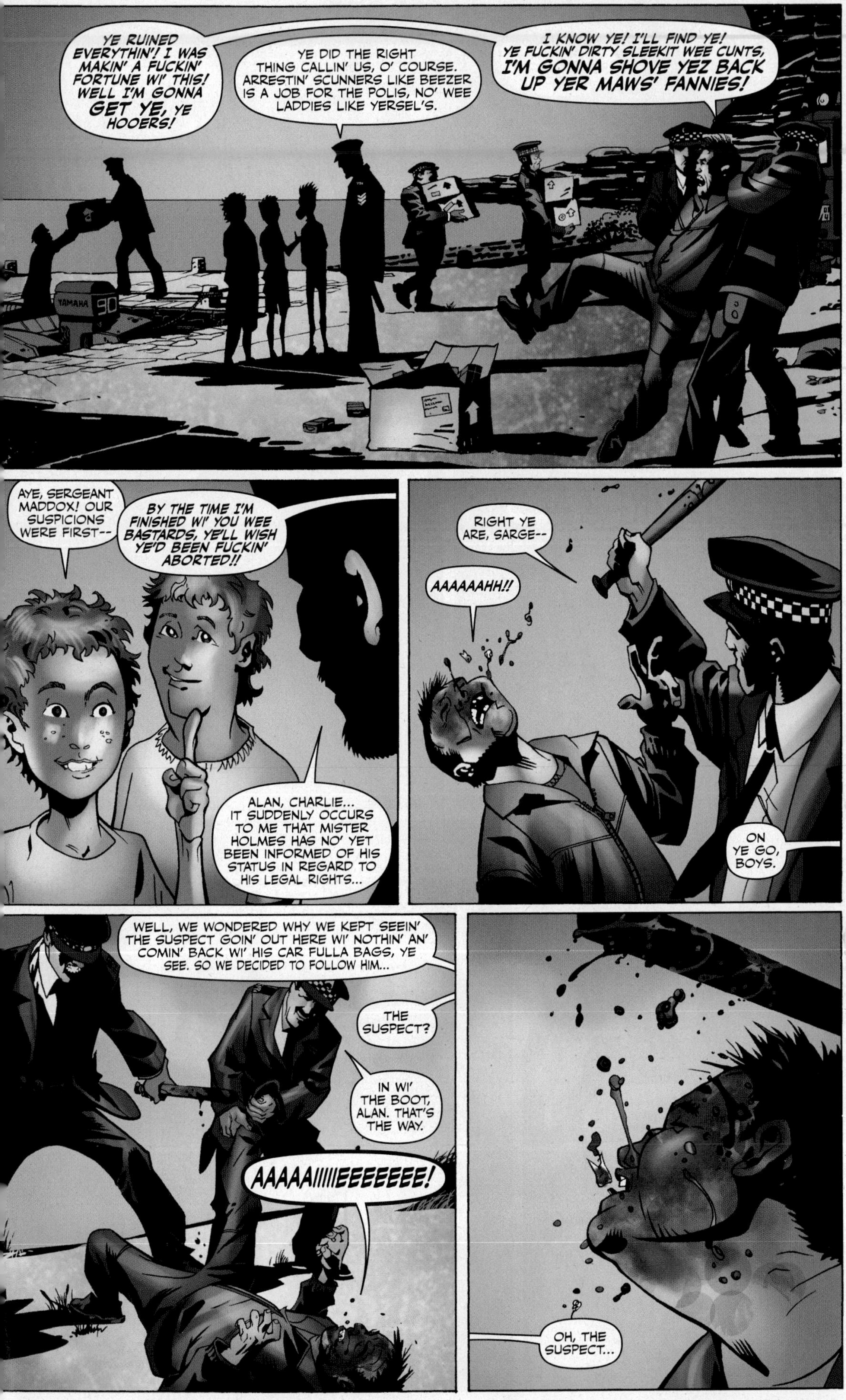
YE RUINED EVERYTHIN'! I WAS MAKIN' A FUCKIN' FORTUNE WI' THIS! WELL I'M GONNA GET YE, YE HOOERS!
YE DID THE RIGHT THING CALLIN' US, O' COURSE. ARRESTIN' SCUNNERS LIKE BEEZER IS A JOB FOR THE POLIS, NO' WEE LADDIES LIKE YERSEL'S.
I KNOW YE! I'LL FIND YE! YE FUCKIN' DIRTY SLEEKIT WEE CUNTS, I'M GONNA SHOVE YEZ BACK UP YER MAWS' FANNIES!
YAMAHA
AYE, SERGEANT MADDOX! OUR SUSPICIONS WERE FIRST--
BY THE TIME I'M FINISHED WI' YOU WEE BASTARDS, YE'LL WISH YE'D BEEN FUCKIN' ABORTED!!
ALAN, CHARLIE... IT SUDDENLY OCCURS TO ME THAT MISTER HOLMES HAS NO' YET BEEN INFORMED OF HIS STATUS IN REGARD TO HIS LEGAL RIGHTS...
RIGHT YE ARE, SARGE--
AAAAAAHH!!
ON YE GO, BOYS.
WELL, WE WONDERED WHY WE KEPT SEEIN' THE SUSPECT GOIN' OUT HERE WI' NOTHIN' AN' COMIN' BACK WI' HIS CAR FULLA BAGS, YE SEE. SO WE DECIDED TO FOLLOW HIM...
THE SUSPECT?
IN WI' THE BOOT, ALAN. THAT'S THE WAY.
AAAAAIIIIIEEEEEEE!
OH, THE SUSPECT...

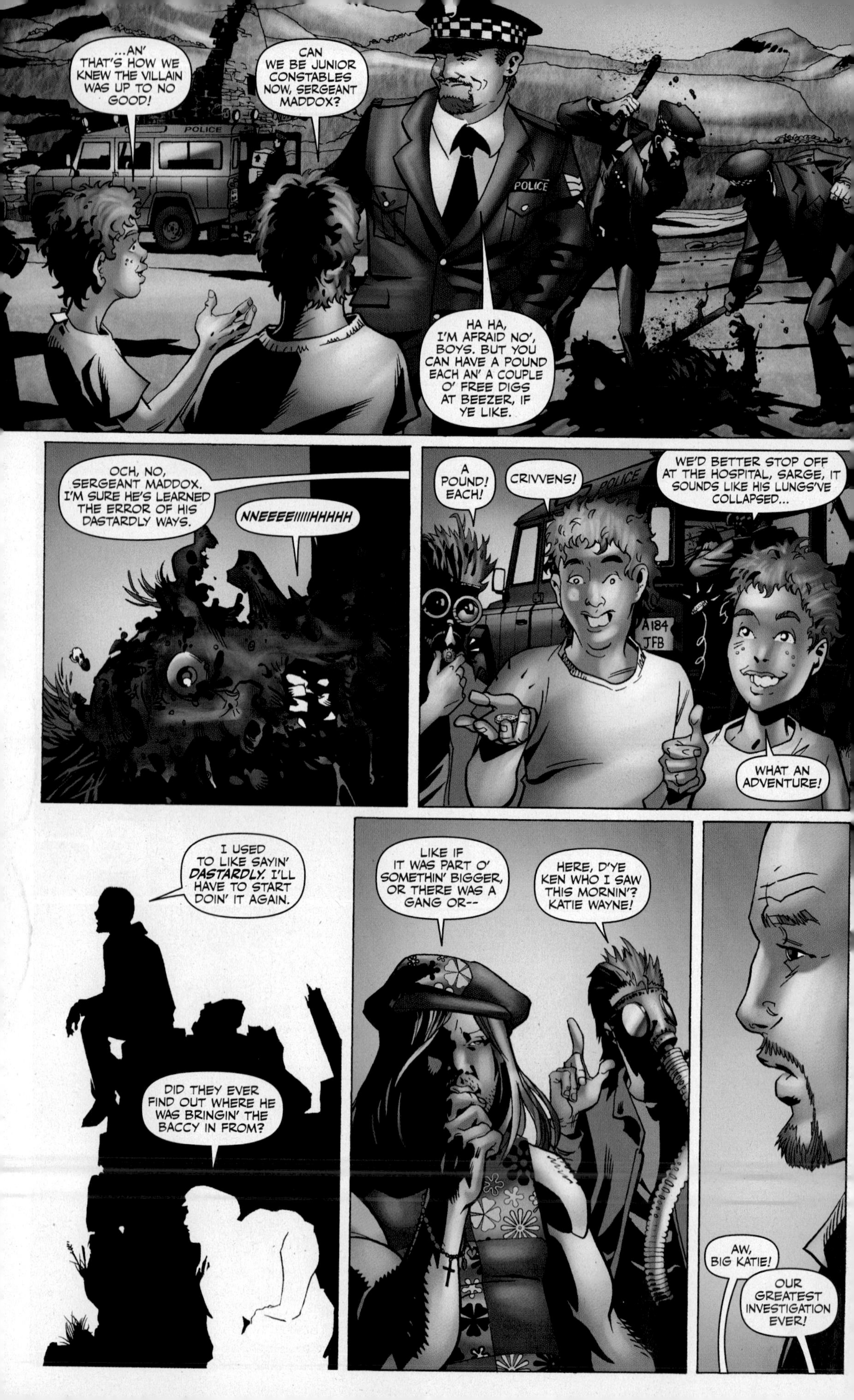
...AN' THAT'S HOW WE KNEW THE VILLAIN WAS UP TO NO GOOD!
CAN WE BE JUNIOR CONSTABLES NOW, SERGEANT MADDOX?
POLICE
POLICE
HA HA, I'M AFRAID NO', BOYS. BUT YOU CAN HAVE A POUND EACH AN' A COUPLE O' FREE DIGS AT BEEZER, IF YE LIKE.
OCH, NO, SERGEANT MADDOX. I'M SURE HE'S LEARNED THE ERROR OF HIS DASTARDLY WAYS.
NNEEEEIIIIIHHHHH
A POUND! EACH!
CRIVVENS!
WE'D BETTER STOP OFF AT THE HOSPITAL, SARGE, IT SOUNDS LIKE HIS LUNGS'VE COLLAPSED...
POLICE
A184 JFB
WHAT AN ADVENTURE!
I USED TO LIKE SAYIN' DASTARDLY. I'LL HAVE TO START DOIN' IT AGAIN.
DID THEY EVER FIND OUT WHERE HE WAS BRINGIN' THE BACCY IN FROM?
LIKE IF IT WAS PART O' SOMETHIN' BIGGER, OR THERE WAS A GANG OR--
HERE, D'YE KEN WHO I SAW THIS MORNIN'? KATIE WAYNE!
AW, BIG KATIE!
OUR GREATEST INVESTIGATION EVER!

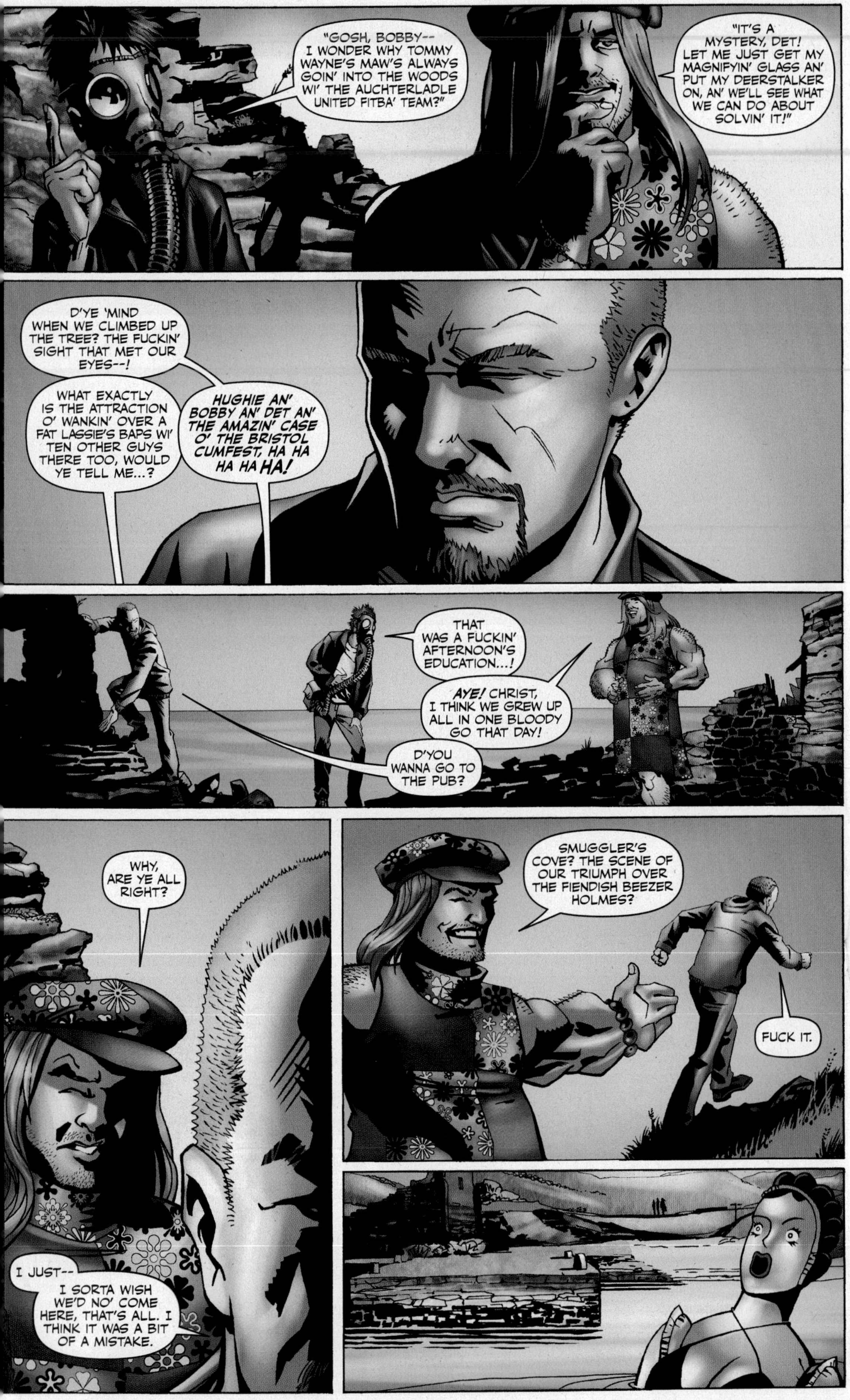
"GOSH, BOBBY-- I WONDER WHY TOMMY WAYNE'S MAW'S ALWAYS GOIN' INTO THE WOODS WI' THE AUCHTERLADLE UNITED FITBA' TEAM?"
"IT'S A MYSTERY, DET! LET ME JUST GET MY MAGNIFYIN' GLASS AN' PUT MY DEERSTALKER ON, AN' WE'LL SEE WHAT WE CAN DO ABOUT SOLVIN' IT!"
D'YE 'MIND WHEN WE CLIMBED UP THE TREE? THE FUCKIN' SIGHT THAT MET OUR EYES--!
HUGHIE AN' BOBBY AN' DET AN' THE AMAZIN' CASE O' THE BRISTOL CUMFEST, HA HA HA HA HA!
WHAT EXACTLY IS THE ATTRACTION O' WANKIN' OVER A FAT LASSIE'S BAPS WI' TEN OTHER GUYS THERE TOO, WOULD YE TELL ME...?
THAT WAS A FUCKIN' AFTERNOON'S EDUCATION...!
AYE! CHRIST, I THINK WE GREW UP ALL IN ONE BLOODY GO THAT DAY!
D'YOU WANNA GO TO THE PUB?
WHY, ARE YE ALL RIGHT?
I JUST--
I SORTA WISH WE'D NO' COME HERE, THAT'S ALL. I THINK IT WAS A BIT OF A MISTAKE.
SMUGGLER'S COVE? THE SCENE OF OUR TRIUMPH OVER THE FIENDISH BEEZER HOLMES?
FUCK IT.

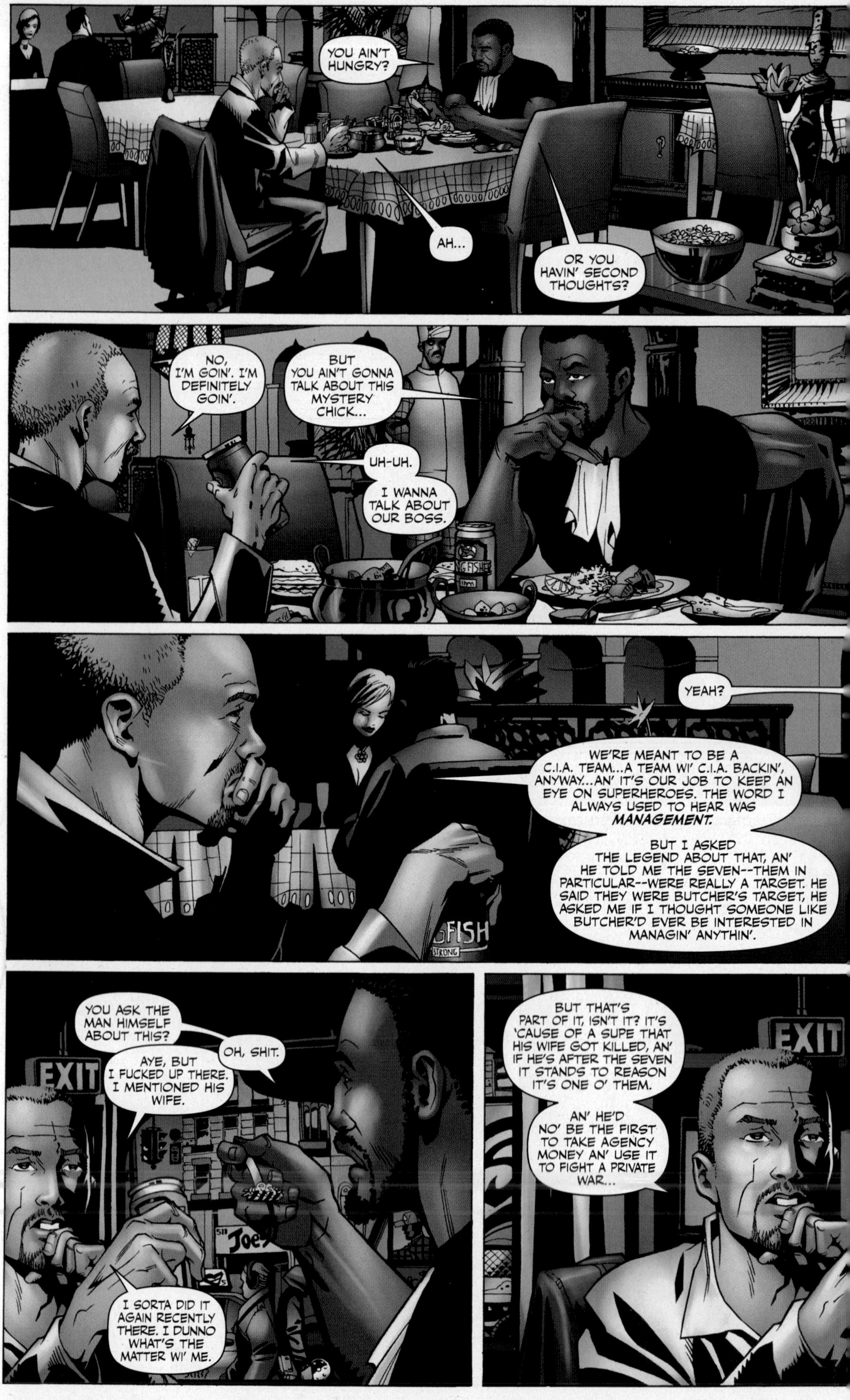
YOU AIN'T HUNGRY?
AH...
OR YOU HAVIN' SECOND THOUGHTS?
NO, I'M GOIN'. I'M DEFINITELY GOIN'.
BUT YOU AIN'T GONNA TALK ABOUT THIS MYSTERY CHICK...
UH-UH.
I WANNA TALK ABOUT OUR BOSS.
YEAH?
WE'RE MEANT TO BE A C.I.A. TEAM...A TEAM WI' C.I.A. BACKIN', ANYWAY...AN' IT'S OUR JOB TO KEEP AN EYE ON SUPERHEROES. THE WORD I ALWAYS USED TO HEAR WAS ***MANAGEMENT.***
BUT I ASKED THE LEGEND ABOUT THAT, AN' HE TOLD ME THE SEVEN--THEM IN PARTICULAR--WERE REALLY A TARGET. HE SAID THEY WERE BUTCHER'S TARGET, HE ASKED ME IF I THOUGHT SOMEONE LIKE BUTCHER'D EVER BE INTERESTED IN MANAGIN' ANYTHIN'.
YOU ASK THE MAN HIMSELF ABOUT THIS?
AYE, BUT I FUCKED UP THERE. I MENTIONED HIS WIFE.
OH, SHIT.
I SORTA DID IT AGAIN RECENTLY THERE. I DUNNO WHAT'S THE MATTER WI' ME.
BUT THAT'S PART OF IT, ISN'T IT? IT'S 'CAUSE OF A SUPE THAT HIS WIFE GOT KILLED, AN' IF HE'S AFTER THE SEVEN IT STANDS TO REASON IT'S ONE O' THEM.
AN' HE'D NO' BE THE FIRST TO TAKE AGENCY MONEY AN' USE IT TO FIGHT A PRIVATE WAR...

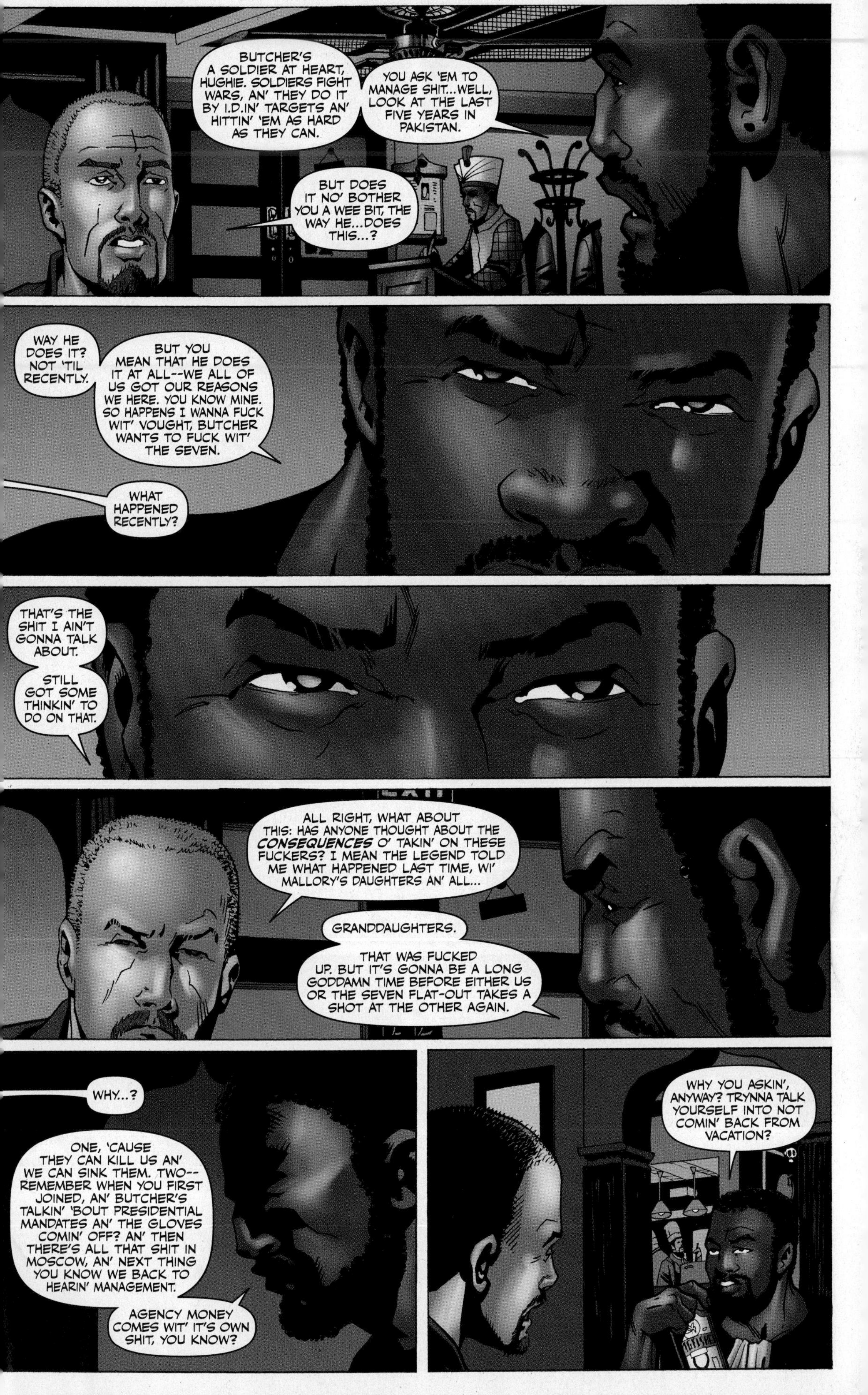
BUTCHER'S A SOLDIER AT HEART, HUGHIE. SOLDIERS FIGHT WARS, AN' THEY DO IT BY I.D.IN' TARGETS AN' HITTIN' 'EM AS HARD AS THEY CAN.
YOU ASK 'EM TO MANAGE SHIT...WELL, LOOK AT THE LAST FIVE YEARS IN PAKISTAN.
BUT DOES IT NO' BOTHER YOU A WEE BIT, THE WAY HE...DOES THIS...?
WAY HE DOES IT? NOT 'TIL RECENTLY.
BUT YOU MEAN THAT HE DOES IT AT ALL--WE ALL OF US GOT OUR REASONS WE HERE. YOU KNOW MINE. SO HAPPENS I WANNA FUCK WIT' VOUGHT, BUTCHER WANTS TO FUCK WIT' THE SEVEN.
WHAT HAPPENED RECENTLY?
THAT'S THE SHIT I AIN'T GONNA TALK ABOUT.
STILL GOT SOME THINKIN' TO DO ON THAT.
ALL RIGHT, WHAT ABOUT THIS: HAS ANYONE THOUGHT ABOUT THE *CONSEQUENCES* O' TAKIN' ON THESE FUCKERS? I MEAN THE LEGEND TOLD ME WHAT HAPPENED LAST TIME, WI' MALLORY'S DAUGHTERS AN' ALL...
GRANDDAUGHTERS.
THAT WAS FUCKED UP. BUT IT'S GONNA BE A LONG GODDAMN TIME BEFORE EITHER US OR THE SEVEN FLAT-OUT TAKES A SHOT AT THE OTHER AGAIN.
WHY...?
ONE, 'CAUSE THEY CAN KILL US AN' WE CAN SINK THEM. TWO-- REMEMBER WHEN YOU FIRST JOINED, AN' BUTCHER'S TALKIN' 'BOUT PRESIDENTIAL MANDATES AN' THE GLOVES COMIN' OFF? AN' THEN THERE'S ALL THAT SHIT IN MOSCOW, AN' NEXT THING YOU KNOW WE BACK TO HEARIN' MANAGEMENT.
AGENCY MONEY COMES WIT' IT'S OWN SHIT, YOU KNOW?
WHY YOU ASKIN', ANYWAY? TRYNNA TALK YOURSELF INTO NOT COMIN' BACK FROM VACATION?

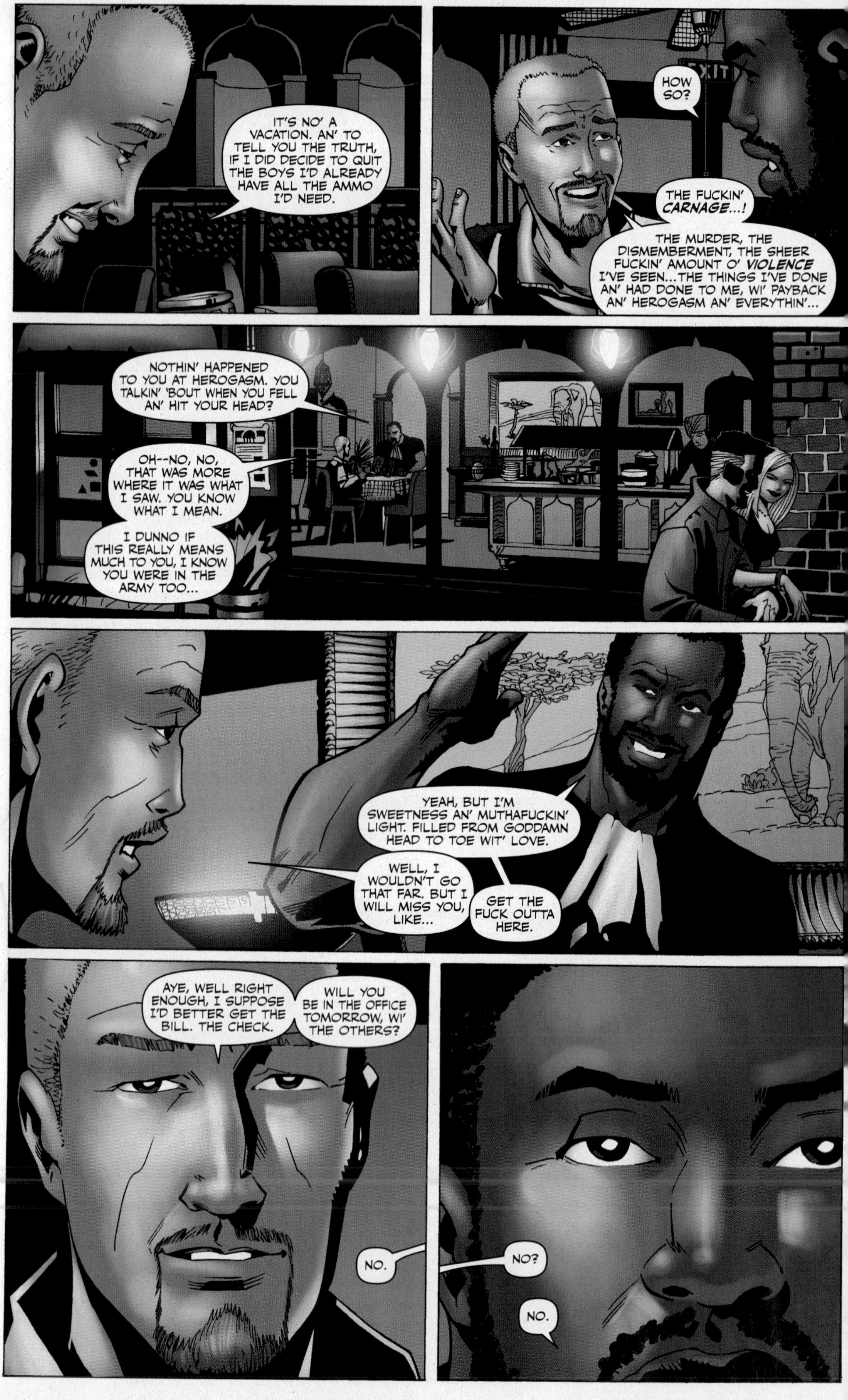
IT'S NO' A VACATION. AN' TO TELL YOU THE TRUTH, IF I DID DECIDE TO QUIT THE BOYS I'D ALREADY HAVE ALL THE AMMO I'D NEED.
HOW SO?
THE FUCKIN' *CARNAGE*...!
THE MURDER, THE DISMEMBERMENT, THE SHEER FUCKIN' AMOUNT O' *VIOLENCE* I'VE SEEN...THE THINGS I'VE DONE AN' HAD DONE TO ME, WI' PAYBACK AN' HEROGASM AN' EVERYTHIN'...
NOTHIN' HAPPENED TO YOU AT HEROGASM. YOU TALKIN' 'BOUT WHEN YOU FELL AN' HIT YOUR HEAD?
OH--NO, NO, THAT WAS MORE WHERE IT WAS WHAT I SAW. YOU KNOW WHAT I MEAN.
I DUNNO IF THIS REALLY MEANS MUCH TO YOU, I KNOW YOU WERE IN THE ARMY TOO...
YEAH, BUT I'M SWEETNESS AN' MUTHAFUCKIN' LIGHT. FILLED FROM GODDAMN HEAD TO TOE WIT' LOVE.
WELL, I WOULDN'T GO THAT FAR. BUT I WILL MISS YOU, LIKE...
GET THE FUCK OUTTA HERE.
AYE, WELL RIGHT ENOUGH, I SUPPOSE I'D BETTER GET THE BILL. THE CHECK.
WILL YOU BE IN THE OFFICE TOMORROW, WI' THE OTHERS?
NO.
NO?
NO.

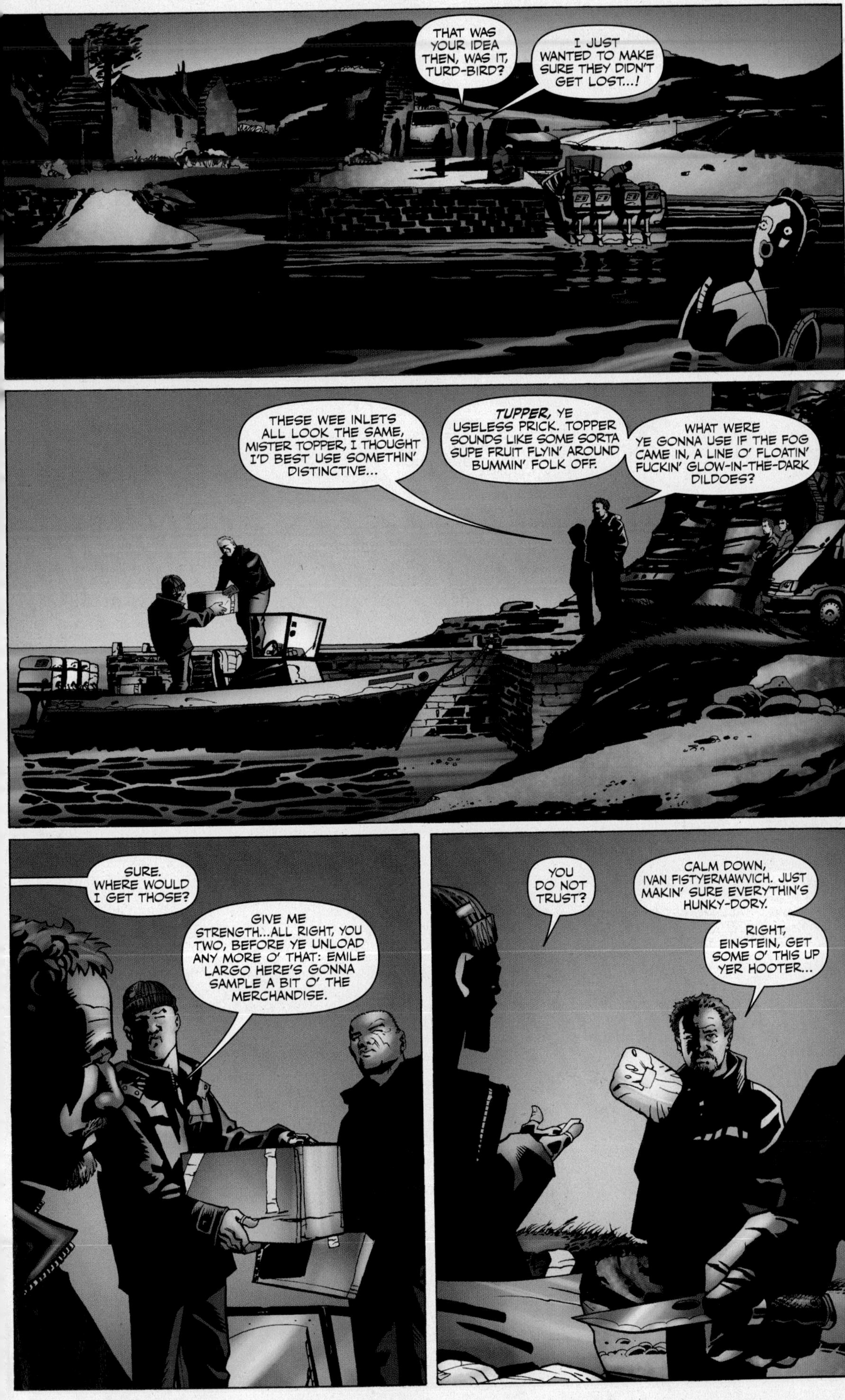
THAT WAS YOUR IDEA THEN, WAS IT, TURD-BIRD?
I JUST WANTED TO MAKE SURE THEY DIDN'T GET LOST...!
THESE WEE INLETS ALL LOOK THE SAME, MISTER TOPPER, I THOUGHT I'D BEST USE SOMETHIN' DISTINCTIVE...
TUPPER, YE USELESS PRICK. TOPPER SOUNDS LIKE SOME SORTA SUPE FRUIT FLYIN' AROUND BUMMIN' FOLK OFF.
WHAT WERE YE GONNA USE IF THE FOG CAME IN, A LINE O' FLOATIN' FUCKIN' GLOW-IN-THE-DARK DILDOES?
SURE. WHERE WOULD I GET THOSE?
GIVE ME STRENGTH...ALL RIGHT, YOU TWO, BEFORE YE UNLOAD ANY MORE O' THAT: EMILE LARGO HERE'S GONNA SAMPLE A BIT O' THE MERCHANDISE.
YOU DO NOT TRUST?
CALM DOWN, IVAN FISTYERMAWVICH. JUST MAKIN' SURE EVERYTHIN'S HUNKY-DORY.
RIGHT, EINSTEIN, GET SOME O' THIS UP YER HOOTER...

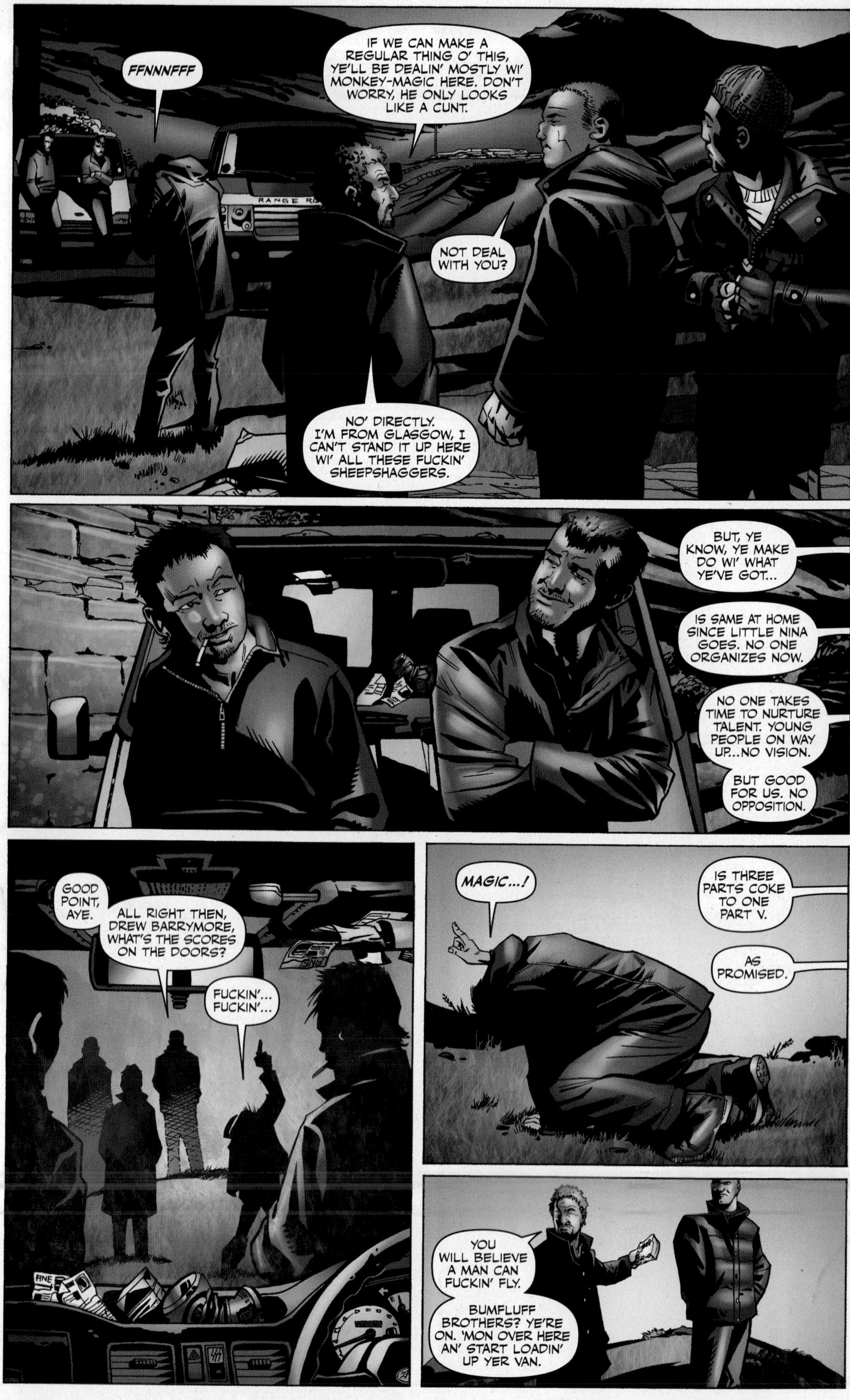
FFNNNFFF
IF WE CAN MAKE A REGULAR THING O' THIS, YE'LL BE DEALIN' MOSTLY WI' MONKEY-MAGIC HERE. DON'T WORRY, HE ONLY LOOKS LIKE A CUNT.
NOT DEAL WITH YOU?
NO' DIRECTLY. I'M FROM GLASGOW, I CAN'T STAND IT UP HERE WI' ALL THESE FUCKIN' SHEEPSHAGGERS.
BUT, YE KNOW, YE MAKE DO WI' WHAT YE'VE GOT...
IS SAME AT HOME SINCE LITTLE NINA GOES. NO ONE ORGANIZES NOW.
NO ONE TAKES TIME TO NURTURE TALENT. YOUNG PEOPLE ON WAY UP...NO VISION.
BUT GOOD FOR US. NO OPPOSITION.
GOOD POINT, AYE.
ALL RIGHT THEN, DREW BARRYMORE, WHAT'S THE SCORES ON THE DOORS?
FUCKIN'... FUCKIN'...
MAGIC...!
IS THREE PARTS COKE TO ONE PART V.
AS PROMISED.
YOU WILL BELIEVE A MAN CAN FUCKIN' FLY.
BUMFLUFF BROTHERS? YE'RE ON. 'MON OVER HERE AN' START LOADIN' UP YER VAN.

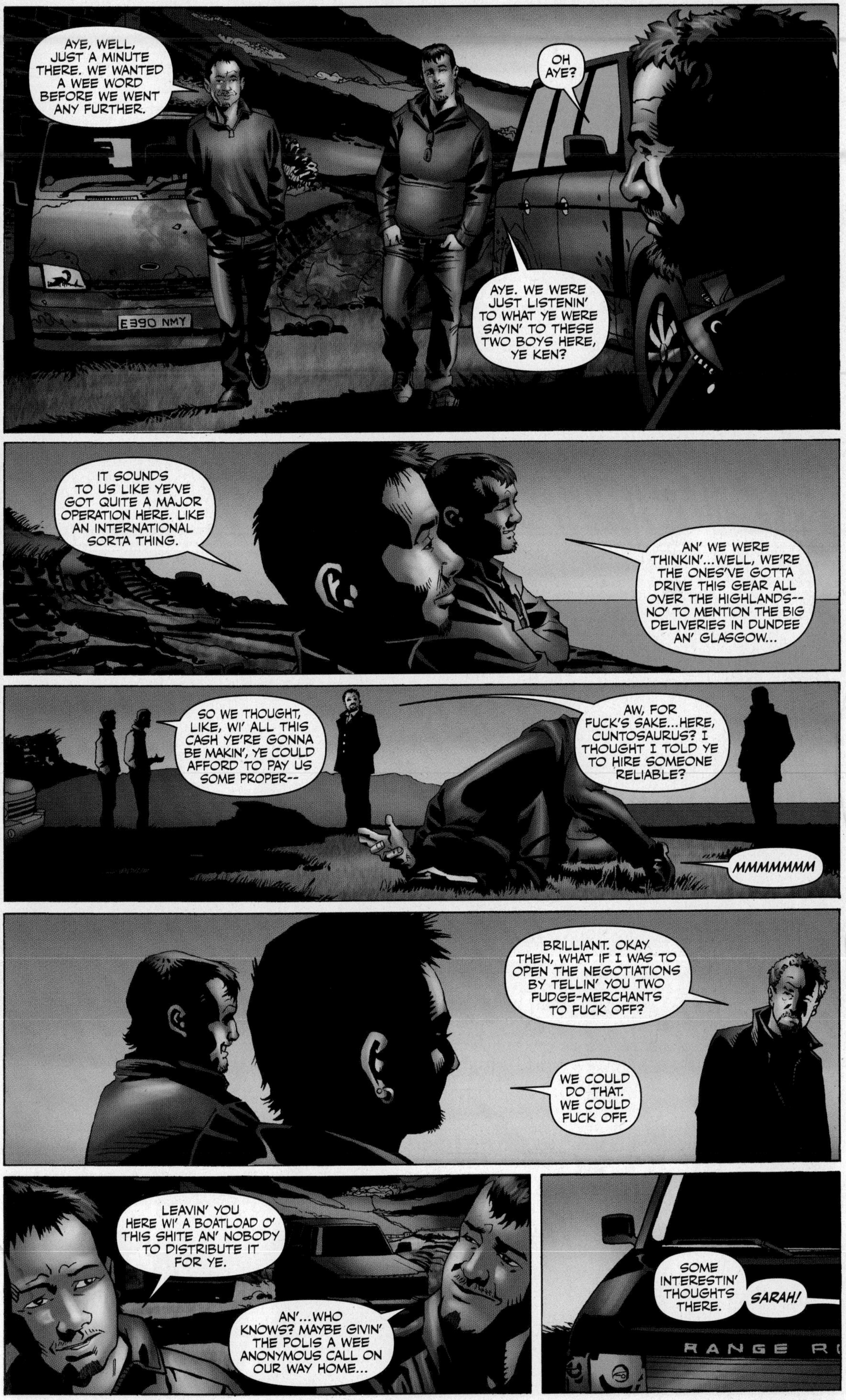

AYE, WELL, JUST A MINUTE THERE. WE WANTED A WEE WORD BEFORE WE WENT ANY FURTHER.
OH AYE?
AYE. WE WERE JUST LISTENIN' TO WHAT YE WERE SAYIN' TO THESE TWO BOYS HERE, YE KEN?
E390 NMY
IT SOUNDS TO US LIKE YE'VE GOT QUITE A MAJOR OPERATION HERE. LIKE AN INTERNATIONAL SORTA THING.
AN' WE WERE THINKIN'...WELL, WE'RE THE ONES'VE GOTTA DRIVE THIS GEAR ALL OVER THE HIGHLANDS--NO' TO MENTION THE BIG DELIVERIES IN DUNDEE AN' GLASGOW...
SO WE THOUGHT, LIKE, WI' ALL THIS CASH YE'RE GONNA BE MAKIN', YE COULD AFFORD TO PAY US SOME PROPER--
AW, FOR FUCK'S SAKE...HERE, CUNTOSAURUS? I THOUGHT I TOLD YE TO HIRE SOMEONE RELIABLE?
MMMMMMM
BRILLIANT. OKAY THEN, WHAT IF I WAS TO OPEN THE NEGOTIATIONS BY TELLIN' YOU TWO FUDGE-MERCHANTS TO FUCK OFF?
WE COULD DO THAT. WE COULD FUCK OFF.
LEAVIN' YOU HERE WI' A BOATLOAD O' THIS SHITE AN' NOBODY TO DISTRIBUTE IT FOR YE.
AN'...WHO KNOWS? MAYBE GIVIN' THE POLIS A WEE ANONYMOUS CALL ON OUR WAY HOME...
SOME INTERESTIN' THOUGHTS THERE.
SARAH!
RANGE RO

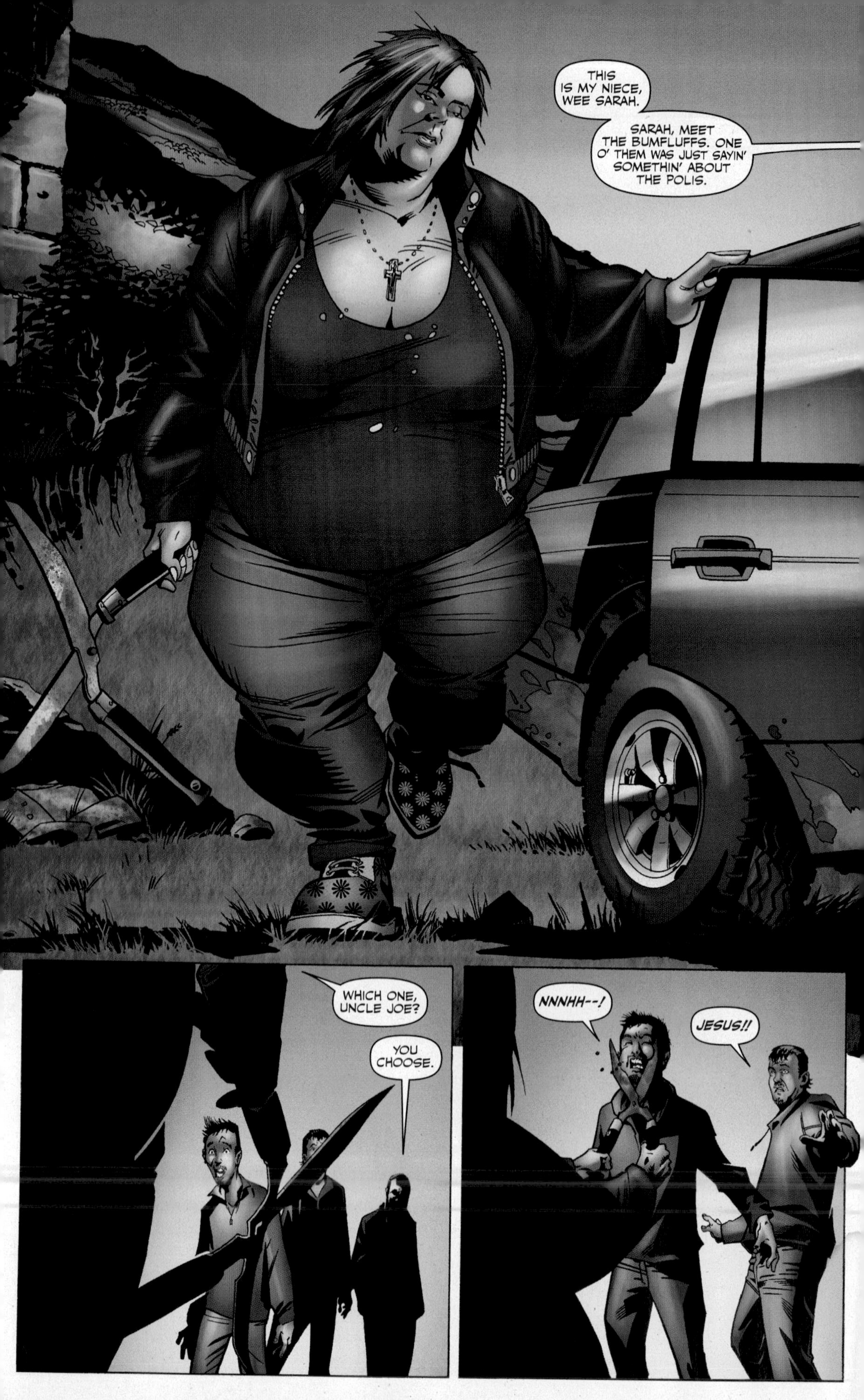
THIS IS MY NIECE, WEE SARAH.
SARAH, MEET THE BUMFLUFFS. ONE O' THEM WAS JUST SAYIN' SOMETHIN' ABOUT THE POLIS.
WHICH ONE, UNCLE JOE?
YOU CHOOSE.
NNNHH--!
JESUS!!

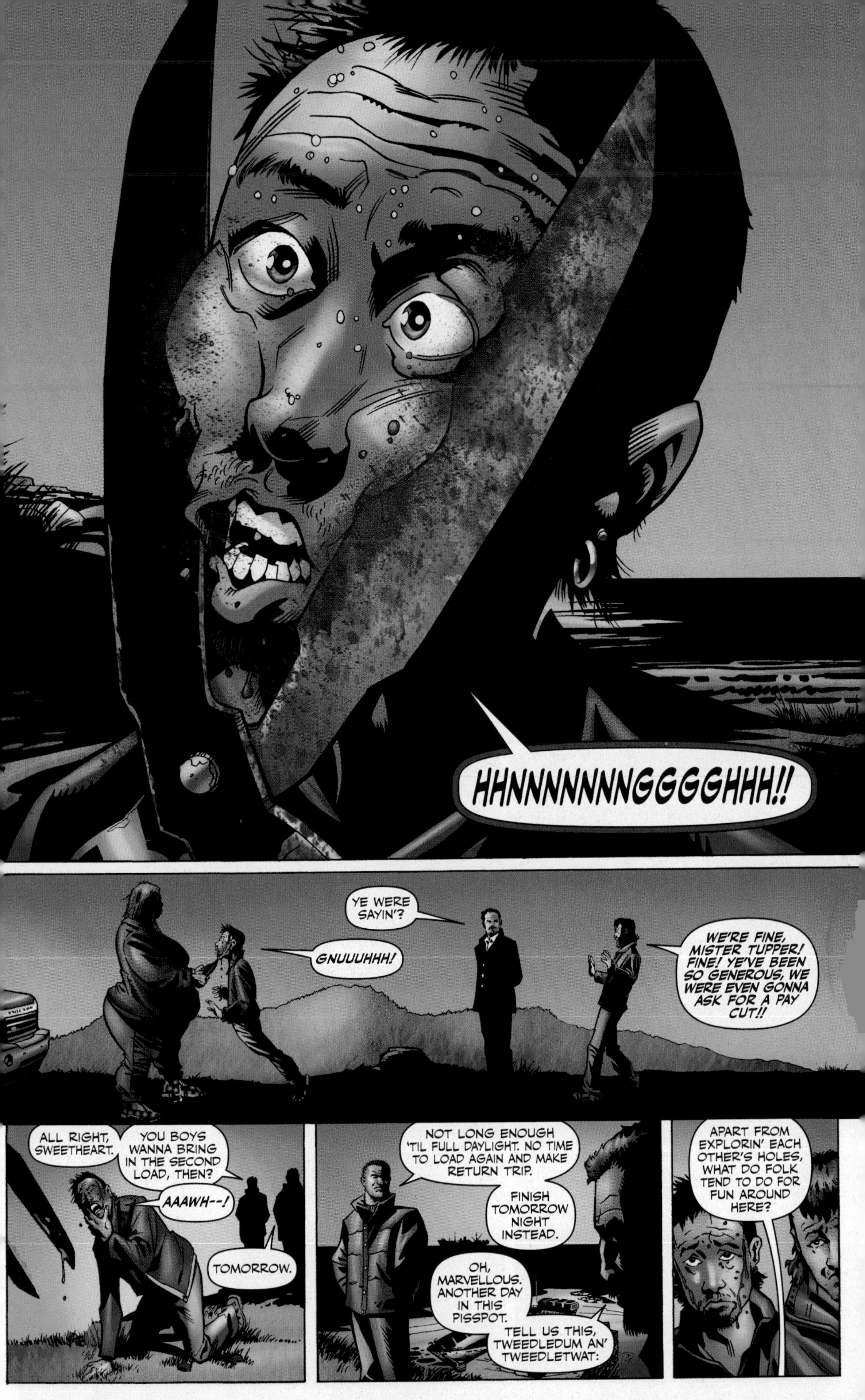
HHNNNNNNNGGGGHHH!!
YE WERE SAYIN'?
GNUUUHHH!
WE'RE FINE, MISTER TUPPER! FINE! YE'VE BEEN SO GENEROUS, WE WERE EVEN GONNA ASK FOR A PAY CUT!!
ALL RIGHT, SWEETHEART.
YOU BOYS WANNA BRING IN THE SECOND LOAD, THEN?
AAAWH--!
TOMORROW.
NOT LONG ENOUGH 'TIL FULL DAYLIGHT. NO TIME TO LOAD AGAIN AND MAKE RETURN TRIP.
FINISH TOMORROW NIGHT INSTEAD.
OH, MARVELLOUS. ANOTHER DAY IN THIS PISSPOT.
TELL US THIS, TWEEDLEDUM AN' TWEEDLETWAT:
APART FROM EXPLORIN' EACH OTHER'S HOLES, WHAT DO FOLK TEND TO DO FOR FUN AROUND HERE?

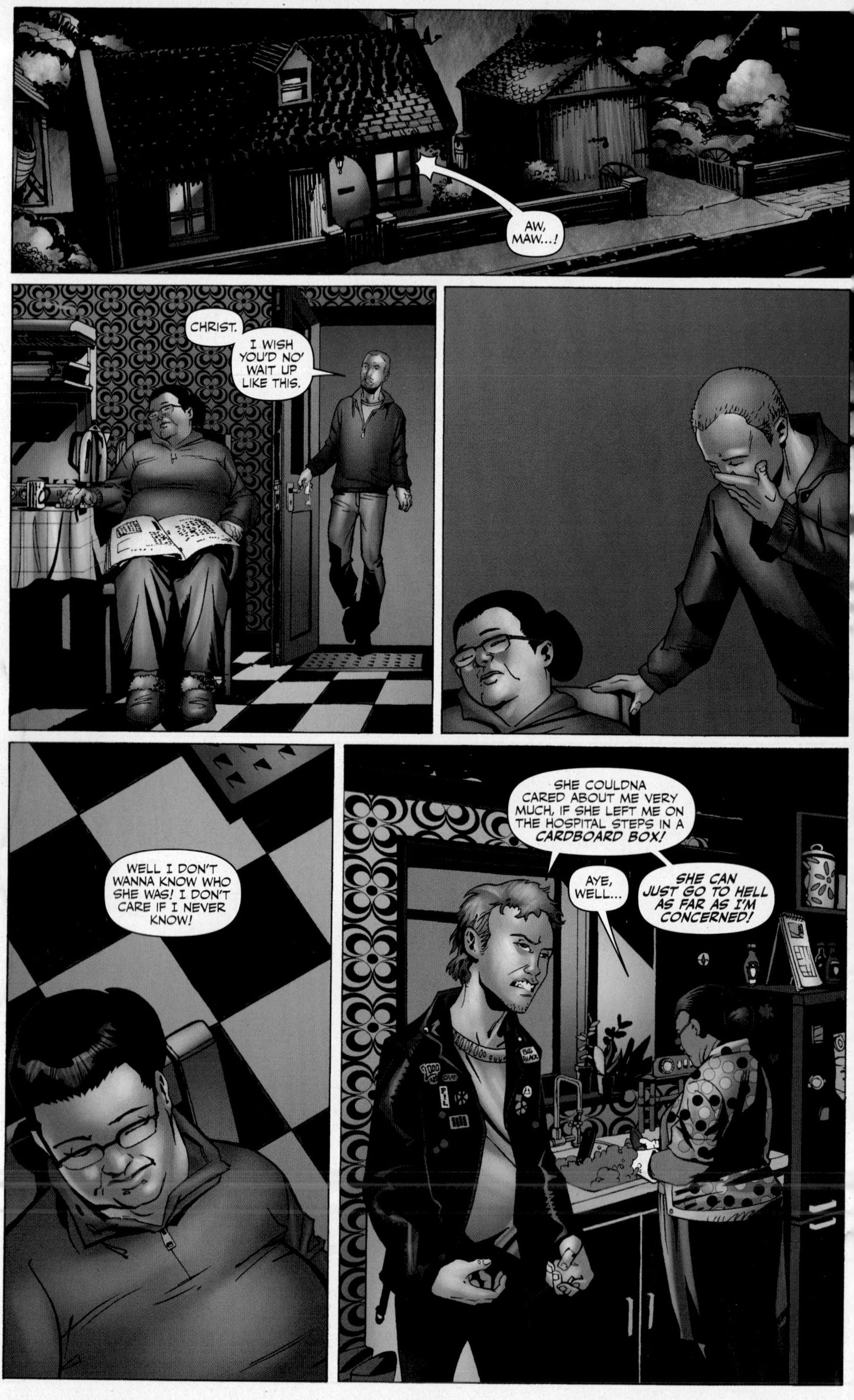
AW, MAW...!
CHRIST.
I WISH YOU'D NO' WAIT UP LIKE THIS.
WELL I DON'T WANNA KNOW WHO SHE WAS! I DON'T CARE IF I NEVER KNOW!
SHE COULDNA CARED ABOUT ME VERY MUCH, IF SHE LEFT ME ON THE HOSPITAL STEPS IN A *CARDBOARD BOX!*
AYE, WELL...
SHE CAN JUST GO TO HELL AS FAR AS I'M CONCERNED!

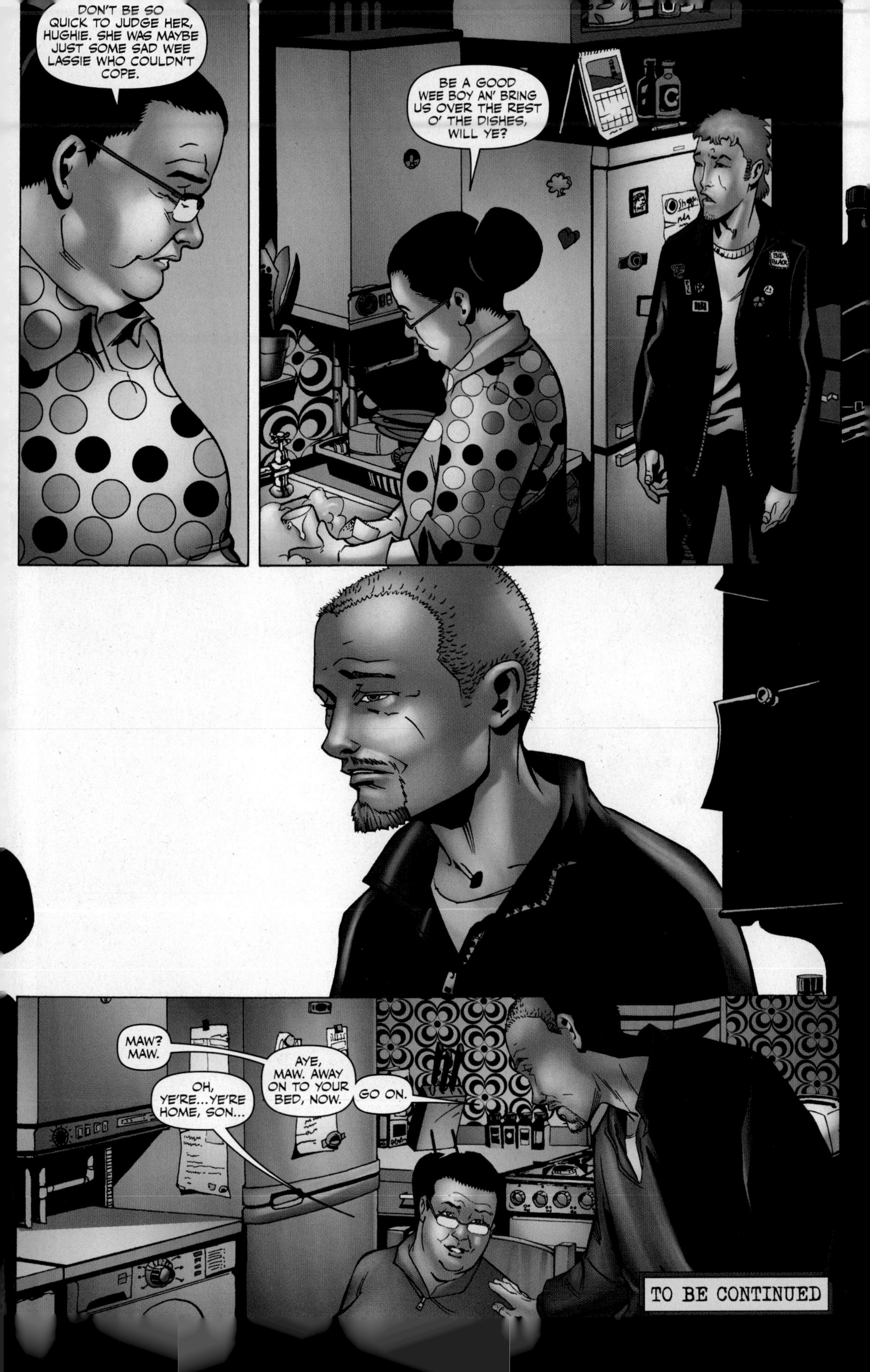
DON'T BE SO QUICK TO JUDGE HER, HUGHIE. SHE WAS MAYBE JUST SOME SAD WEE LASSIE WHO COULDN'T COPE.
BE A GOOD WEE BOY AN' BRING US OVER THE REST O' THE DISHES, WILL YE?
MAW? MAW.
OH, YE'RE...YE'RE HOME, SON...
AYE, MAW. AWAY ON TO YOUR BED, NOW.
GO ON.
TO BE CONTINUED

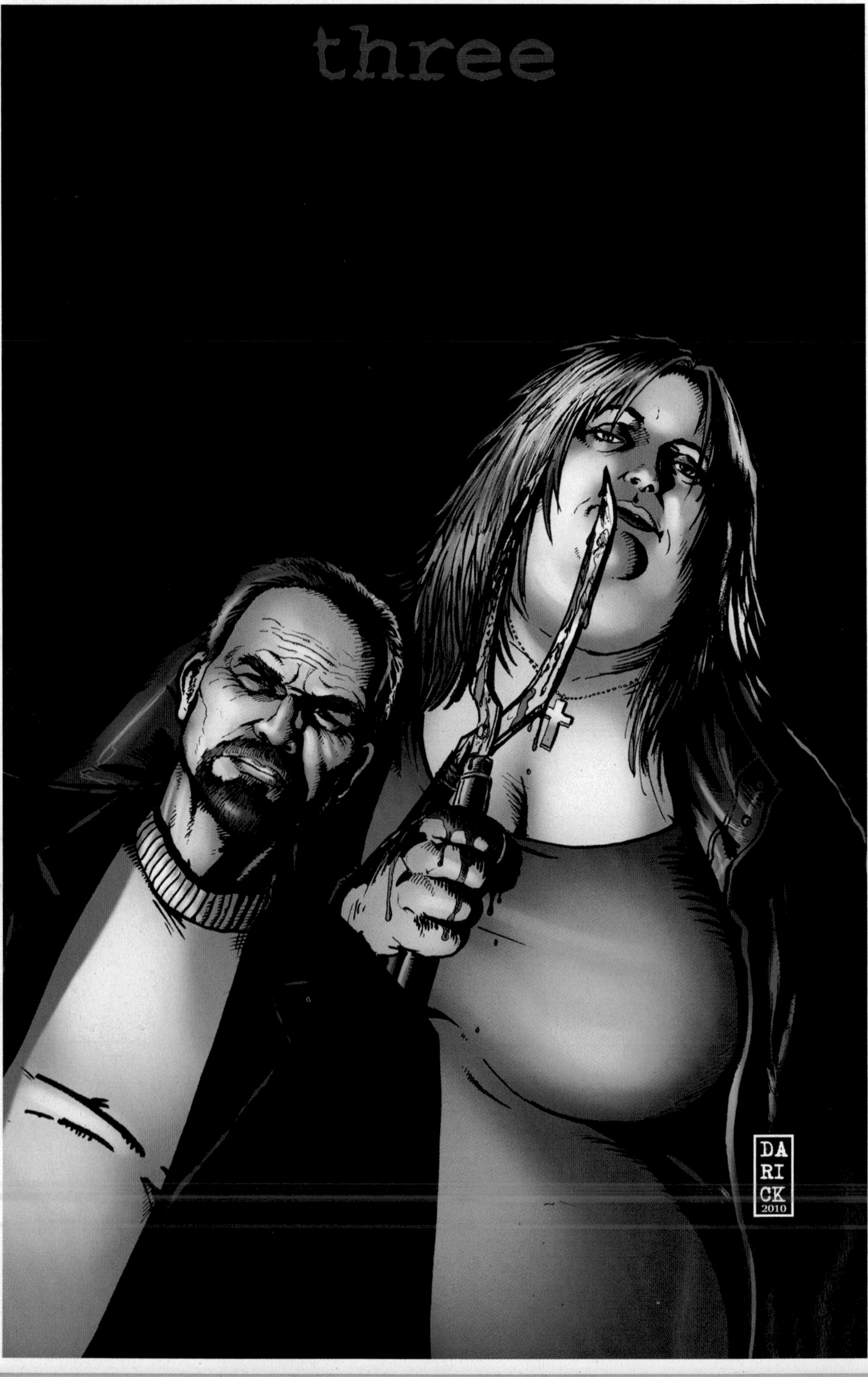
three
DA
RI
CK
2010

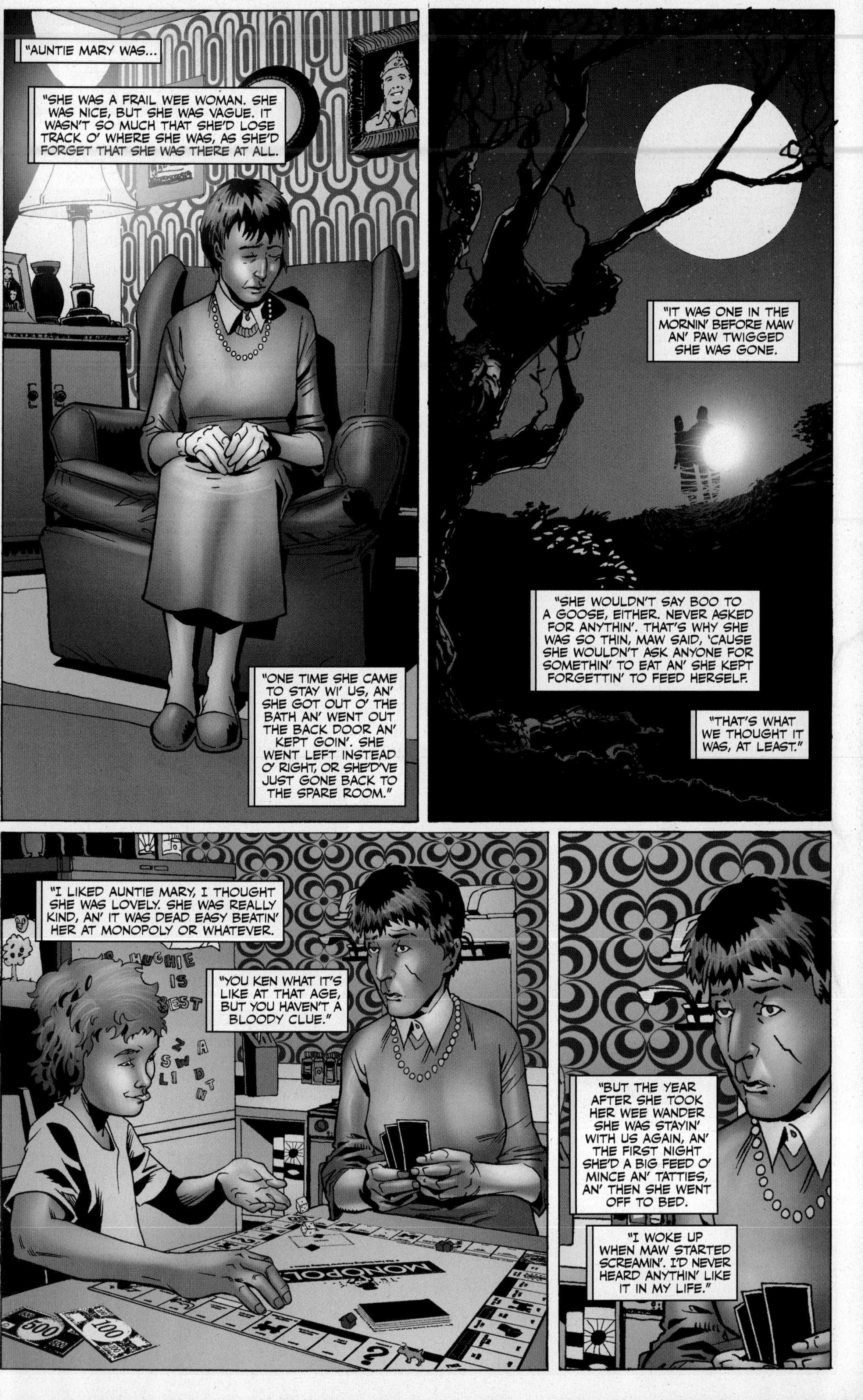
"AUNTIE MARY WAS...
"SHE WAS A FRAIL WEE WOMAN. SHE WAS NICE, BUT SHE WAS VAGUE. IT WASN'T SO MUCH THAT SHE'D LOSE TRACK O' WHERE SHE WAS, AS SHE'D FORGET THAT SHE WAS THERE AT ALL.
"ONE TIME SHE CAME TO STAY WI' US, AN' SHE GOT OUT O' THE BATH AN' WENT OUT THE BACK DOOR AN' KEPT GOIN'. SHE WENT LEFT INSTEAD O' RIGHT, OR SHE'D'VE JUST GONE BACK TO THE SPARE ROOM."
"IT WAS ONE IN THE MORNIN' BEFORE MAW AN' PAW TWIGGED SHE WAS GONE.
"SHE WOULDN'T SAY BOO TO A GOOSE, EITHER. NEVER ASKED FOR ANYTHIN'. THAT'S WHY SHE WAS SO THIN, MAW SAID, 'CAUSE SHE WOULDN'T ASK ANYONE FOR SOMETHIN' TO EAT AN' SHE KEPT FORGETTIN' TO FEED HERSELF.
"THAT'S WHAT WE THOUGHT IT WAS, AT LEAST."
"I LIKED AUNTIE MARY, I THOUGHT SHE WAS LOVELY. SHE WAS REALLY KIND, AN' IT WAS DEAD EASY BEATIN' HER AT MONOPOLY OR WHATEVER.
HUGHIE IS BEST
"YOU KEN WHAT IT'S LIKE AT THAT AGE, BUT YOU HAVEN'T A BLOODY CLUE."
"BUT THE YEAR AFTER SHE TOOK HER WEE WANDER SHE WAS STAYIN' WITH US AGAIN, AN' THE FIRST NIGHT SHE'D A BIG FEED O' MINCE AN' TATTIES, AN' THEN SHE WENT OFF TO BED.
"I WOKE UP WHEN MAW STARTED SCREAMIN'. I'D NEVER HEARD ANYTHIN' LIKE IT IN MY LIFE."

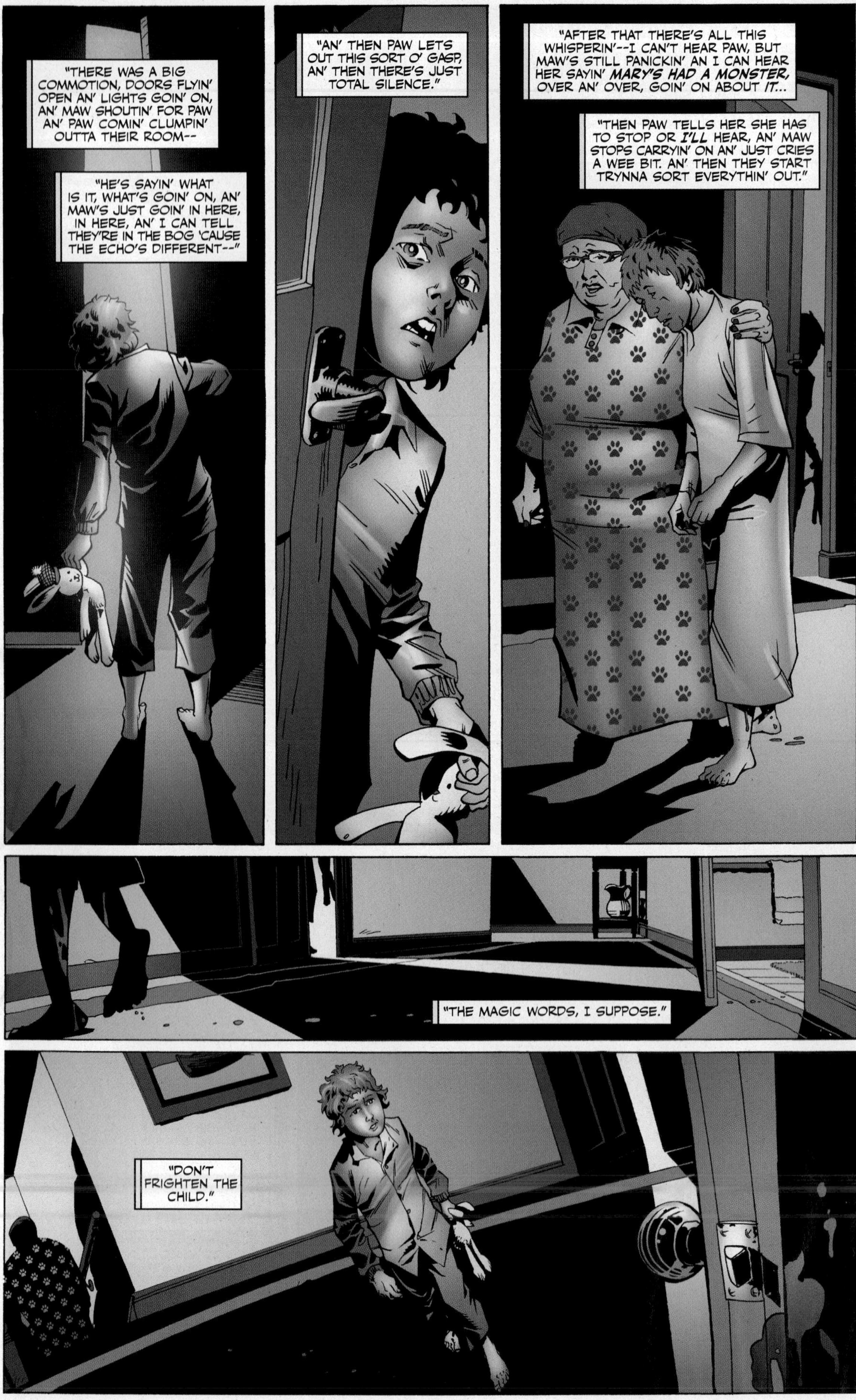
"THERE WAS A BIG COMMOTION, DOORS FLYIN' OPEN AN' LIGHTS GOIN' ON, AN' MAW SHOUTIN' FOR PAW AN' PAW COMIN' CLUMPIN' OUTTA THEIR ROOM--
"HE'S SAYIN' WHAT IS IT, WHAT'S GOIN' ON, AN' MAW'S JUST GOIN' IN HERE, IN HERE, AN' I CAN TELL THEY'RE IN THE BOG 'CAUSE THE ECHO'S DIFFERENT--"
"AN' THEN PAW LETS OUT THIS SORT O' GASP, AN' THEN THERE'S JUST TOTAL SILENCE."
"AFTER THAT THERE'S ALL THIS WHISPERIN'--I CAN'T HEAR PAW, BUT MAW'S STILL PANICKIN' AN I CAN HEAR HER SAYIN' ***MARY'S HAD A MONSTER,*** OVER AN' OVER, GOIN' ON ABOUT ***IT...***
"THEN PAW TELLS HER SHE HAS TO STOP OR ***I'LL*** HEAR, AN' MAW STOPS CARRYIN' ON AN' JUST CRIES A WEE BIT. AN' THEN THEY START TRYNNA SORT EVERYTHIN' OUT."
"THE MAGIC WORDS, I SUPPOSE."
"DON'T FRIGHTEN THE CHILD."

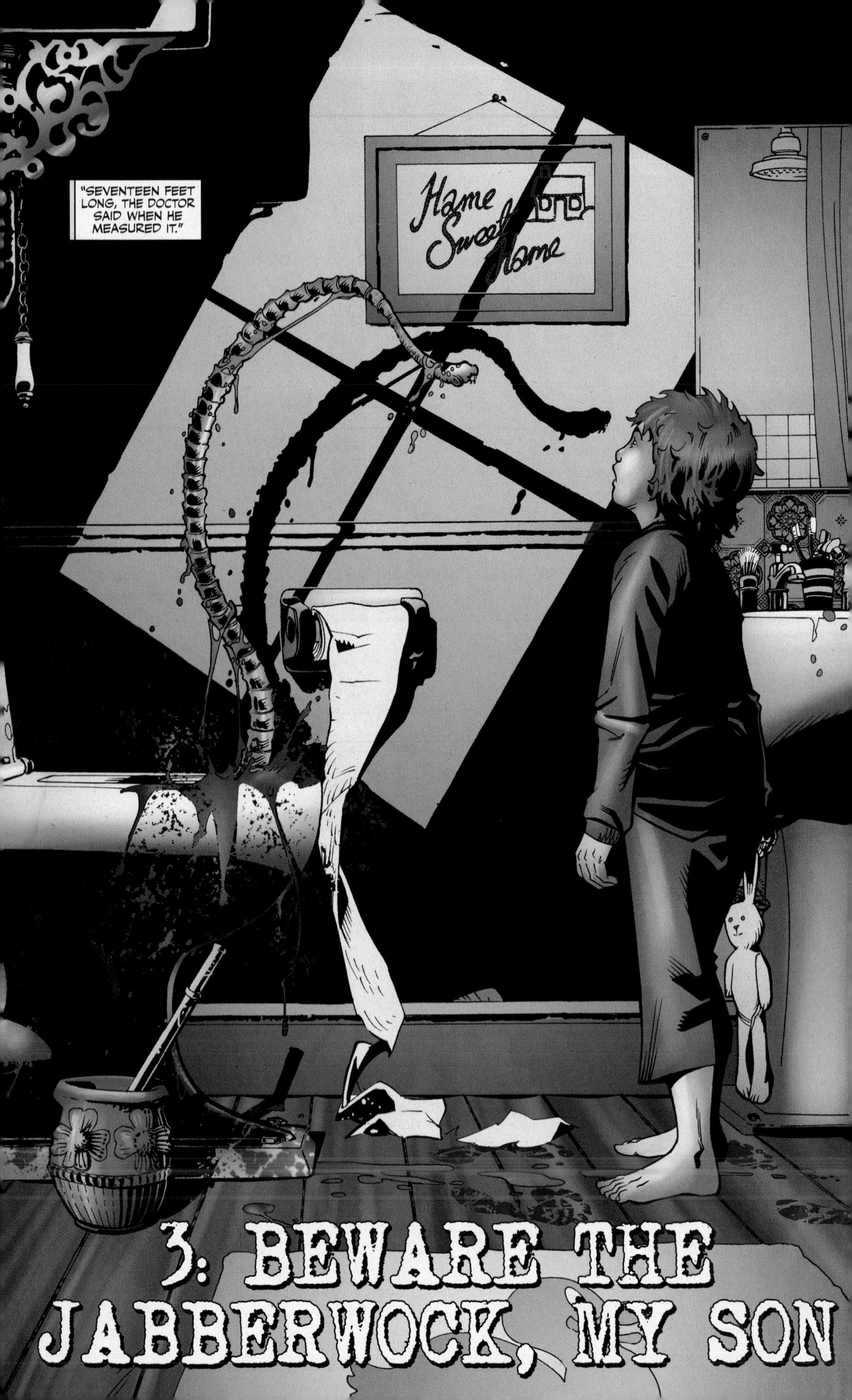
"SEVENTEEN FEET LONG, THE DOCTOR SAID WHEN HE MEASURED IT."
3: BEWARE THE JABBERWOCK, MY SON

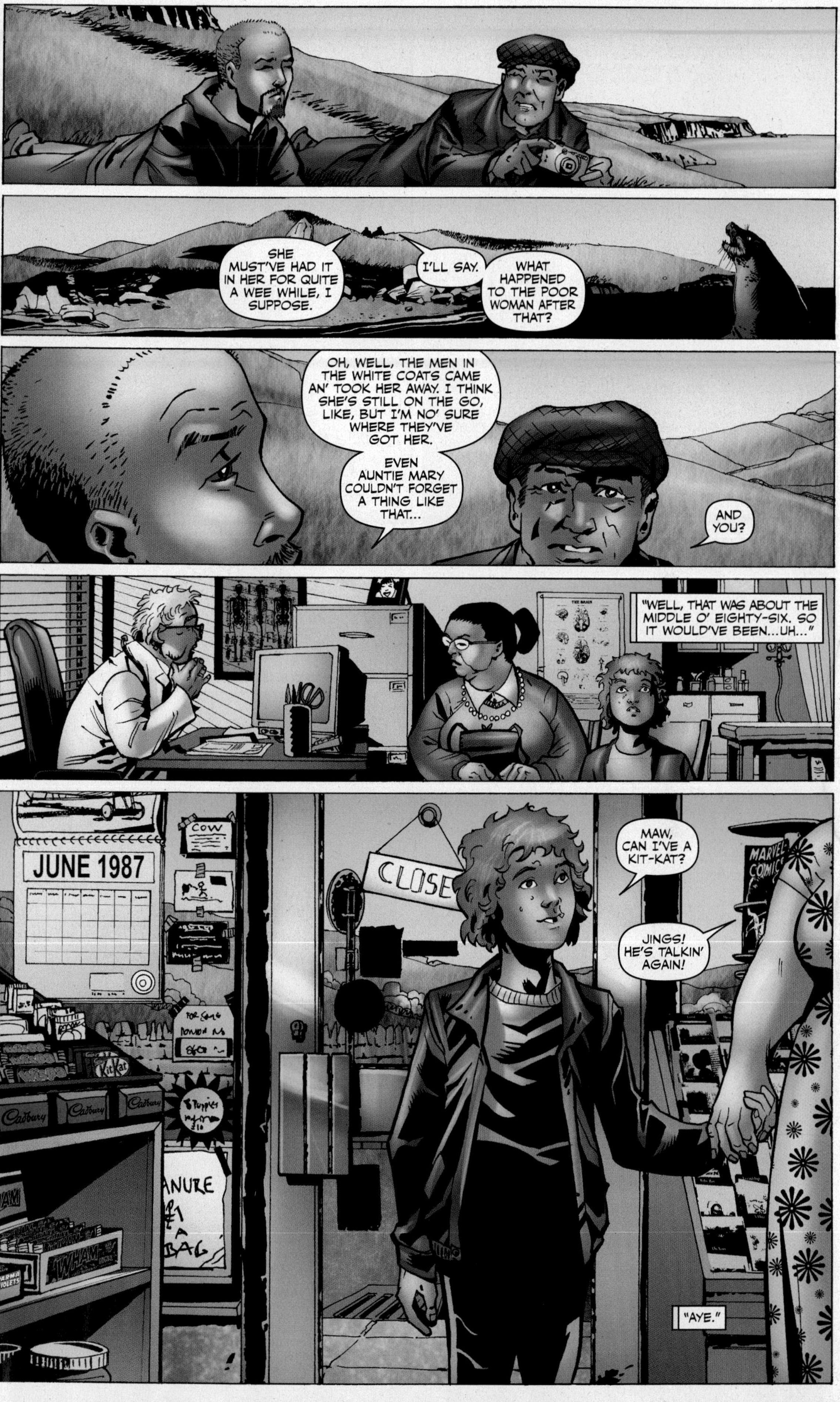
SHE MUST'VE HAD IT IN HER FOR QUITE A WEE WHILE, I SUPPOSE.
I'LL SAY.
WHAT HAPPENED TO THE POOR WOMAN AFTER THAT?
OH, WELL, THE MEN IN THE WHITE COATS CAME AN' TOOK HER AWAY. I THINK SHE'S STILL ON THE GO, LIKE, BUT I'M NO' SURE WHERE THEY'VE GOT HER.
EVEN AUNTIE MARY COULDN'T FORGET A THING LIKE THAT...
AND YOU?
"WELL, THAT WAS ABOUT THE MIDDLE O' EIGHTY-SIX. SO IT WOULD'VE BEEN...UH..."
COW
JUNE 1987
CLOSE
MARVEL COMICS
Cadbury
WHAM
MAW, CAN I'VE A KIT-KAT?
JINGS! HE'S TALKIN' AGAIN!
"AYE."

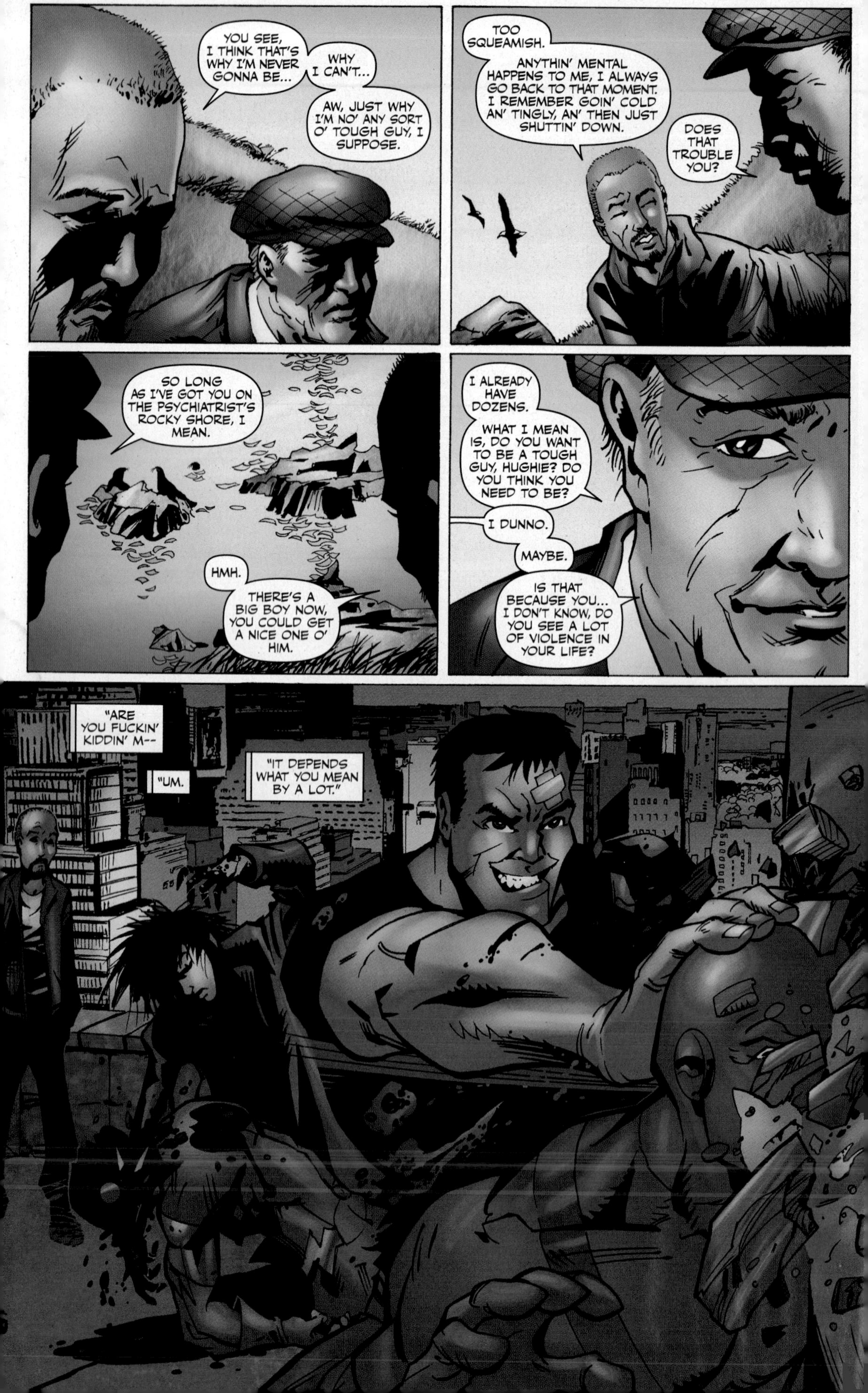
YOU SEE, I THINK THAT'S WHY I'M NEVER GONNA BE...
WHY I CAN'T...
AW, JUST WHY I'M NO' ANY SORT O' TOUGH GUY, I SUPPOSE.
TOO SQUEAMISH.
ANYTHIN' MENTAL HAPPENS TO ME, I ALWAYS GO BACK TO THAT MOMENT. I REMEMBER GOIN' COLD AN' TINGLY, AN' THEN JUST SHUTTIN' DOWN.
DOES THAT TROUBLE YOU?
SO LONG AS I'VE GOT YOU ON THE PSYCHIATRIST'S ROCKY SHORE, I MEAN.
HMH.
THERE'S A BIG BOY NOW, YOU COULD GET A NICE ONE O' HIM.
I ALREADY HAVE DOZENS.
WHAT I MEAN IS, DO YOU WANT TO BE A TOUGH GUY, HUGHIE? DO YOU THINK YOU NEED TO BE?
I DUNNO.
MAYBE.
IS THAT BECAUSE YOU... I DON'T KNOW, DO YOU SEE A LOT OF VIOLENCE IN YOUR LIFE?
"ARE YOU FUCKIN' KIDDIN' M--
"UM.
"IT DEPENDS WHAT YOU MEAN BY A LOT."

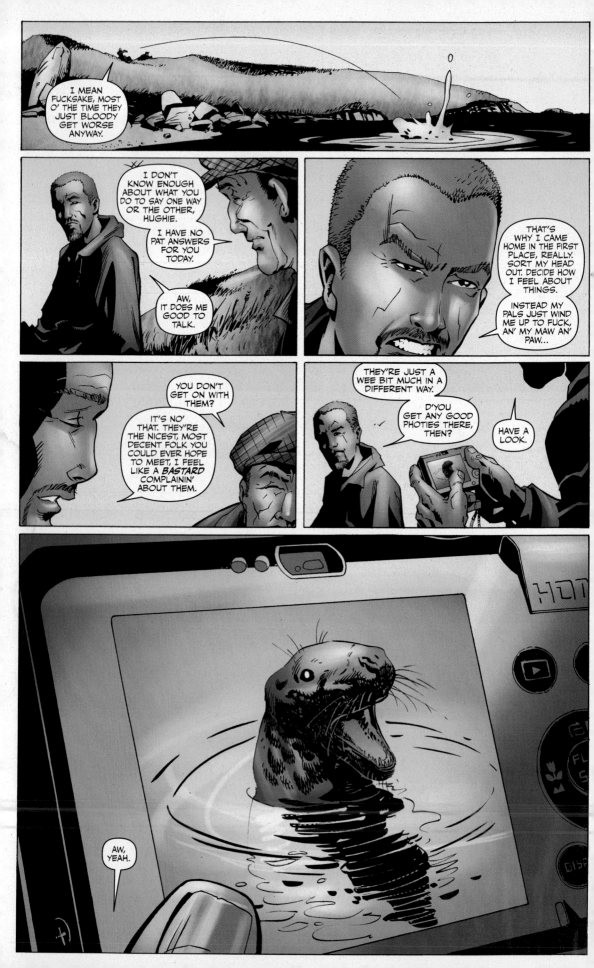

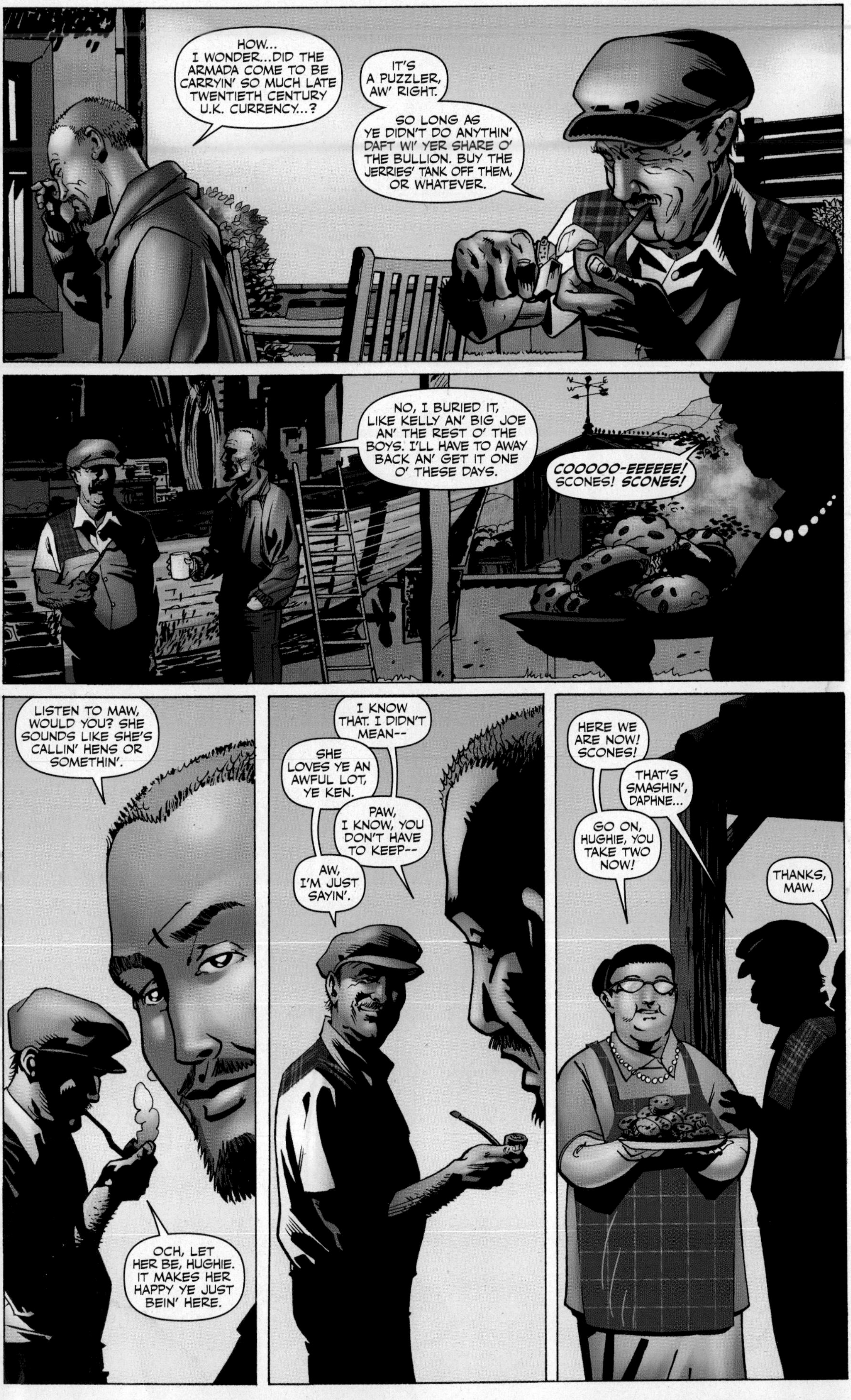
HOW... I WONDER...DID THE ARMADA COME TO BE CARRYIN' SO MUCH LATE TWENTIETH CENTURY U.K. CURRENCY...?
IT'S A PUZZLER, AW' RIGHT.
SO LONG AS YE DIDN'T DO ANYTHIN' DAFT WI' YER SHARE O' THE BULLION. BUY THE JERRIES' TANK OFF THEM, OR WHATEVER.
NO, I BURIED IT, LIKE KELLY AN' BIG JOE AN' THE REST O' THE BOYS. I'LL HAVE TO AWAY BACK AN' GET IT ONE O' THESE DAYS.
COOOOO-EEEEEE! SCONES! SCONES!
LISTEN TO MAW, WOULD YOU? SHE SOUNDS LIKE SHE'S CALLIN' HENS OR SOMETHIN'.
OCH, LET HER BE, HUGHIE. IT MAKES HER HAPPY YE JUST BEIN' HERE.
I KNOW THAT. I DIDN'T MEAN--
SHE LOVES YE AN AWFUL LOT, YE KEN.
PAW, I KNOW, YOU DON'T HAVE TO KEEP--
AW, I'M JUST SAYIN'.
HERE WE ARE NOW! SCONES!
THAT'S SMASHIN', DAPHNE...
GO ON, HUGHIE, YOU TAKE TWO NOW!
THANKS, MAW.

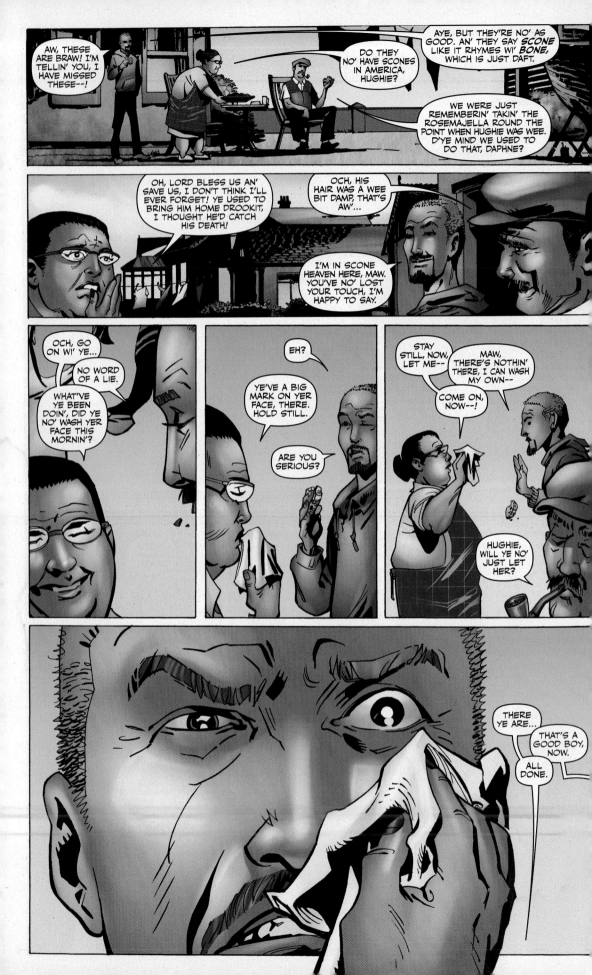

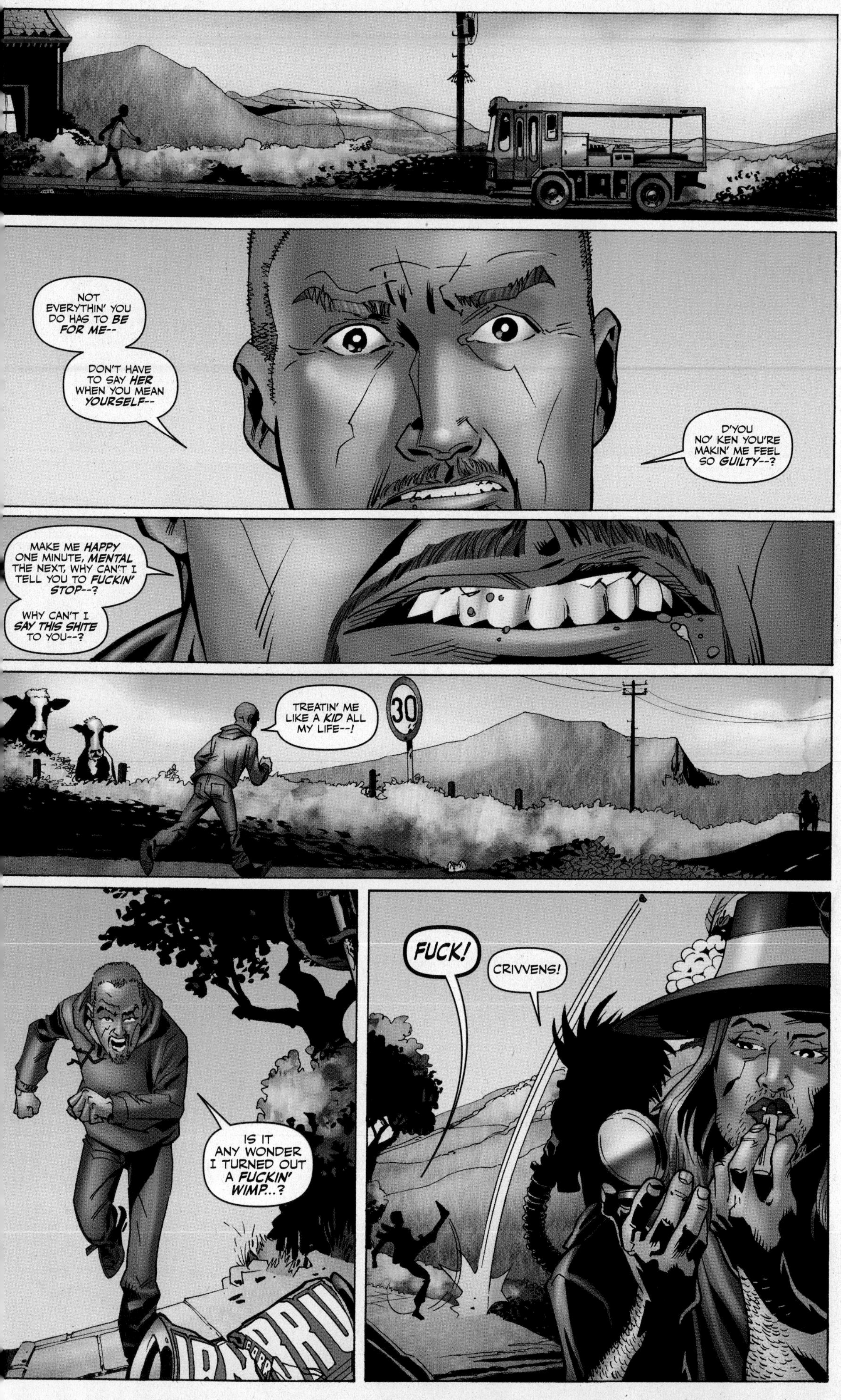
NOT EVERYTHIN' YOU DO HAS TO BE FOR ME--
DON'T HAVE TO SAY HER WHEN YOU MEAN YOURSELF--
D'YOU NO' KEN YOU'RE MAKIN' ME FEEL SO GUILTY--?
MAKE ME HAPPY ONE MINUTE, MENTAL THE NEXT, WHY CAN'T I TELL YOU TO FUCKIN' STOP--?
WHY CAN'T I SAY THIS SHITE TO YOU--?
30
TREATIN' ME LIKE A KID ALL MY LIFE--!
IS IT ANY WONDER I TURNED OUT A FUCKIN' WIMP...?
FUCK!
CRIVVENS!

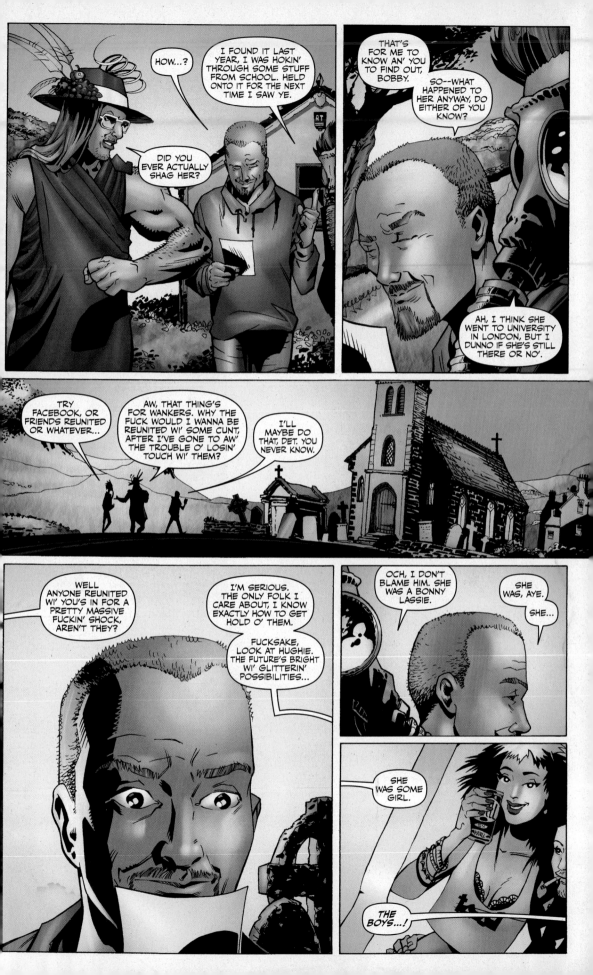

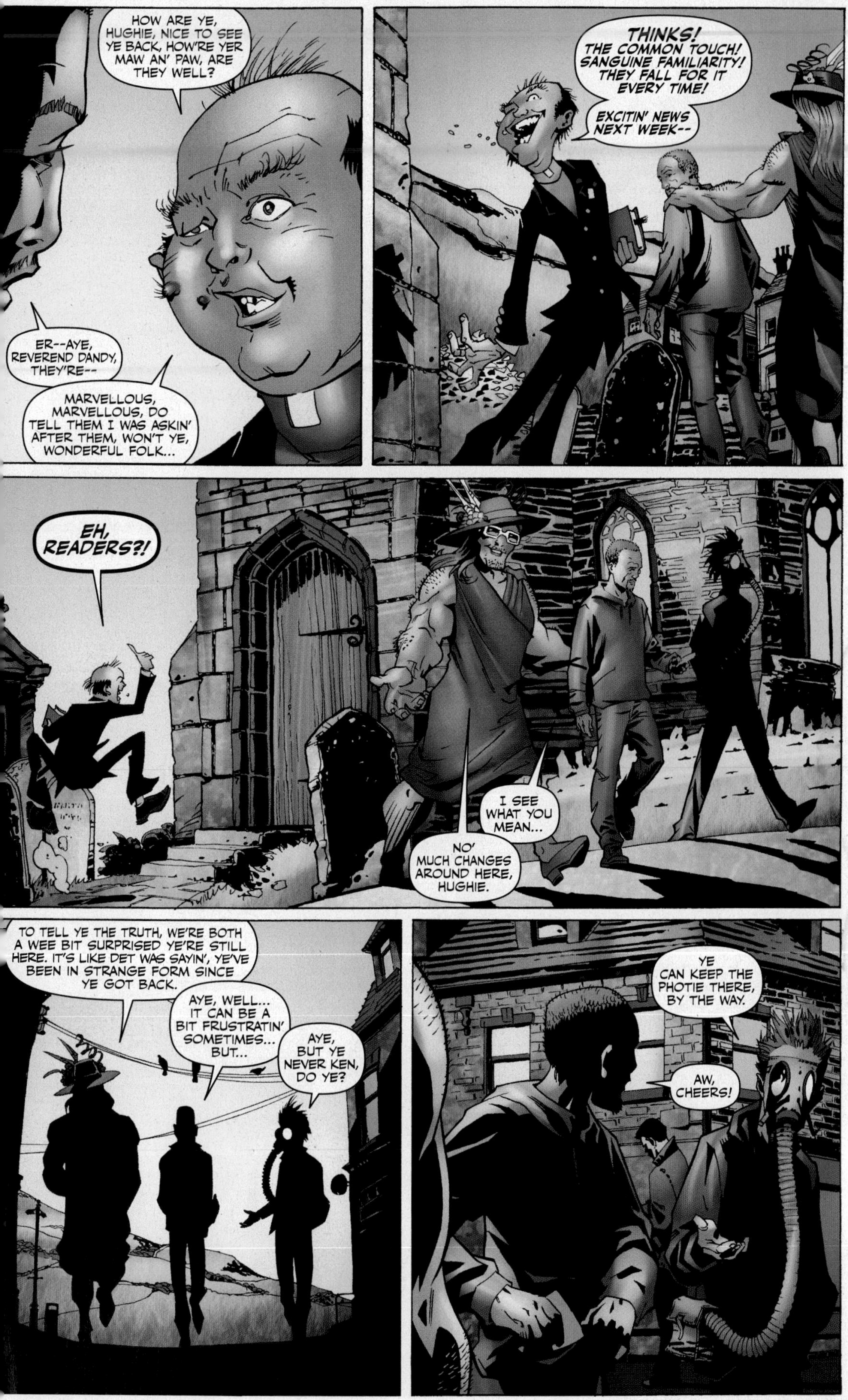
HOW ARE YE, HUGHIE, NICE TO SEE YE BACK, HOW'RE YER MAW AN' PAW, ARE THEY WELL?
ER--AYE, REVEREND DANDY, THEY'RE--
MARVELLOUS, MARVELLOUS, DO TELL THEM I WAS ASKIN' AFTER THEM, WON'T YE, WONDERFUL FOLK...
THINKS! THE COMMON TOUCH! SANGUINE FAMILIARITY! THEY FALL FOR IT EVERY TIME!
EXCITIN' NEWS NEXT WEEK--
EH, READERS?!
I SEE WHAT YOU MEAN...
NO' MUCH CHANGES AROUND HERE, HUGHIE.
TO TELL YE THE TRUTH, WE'RE BOTH A WEE BIT SURPRISED YE'RE STILL HERE. IT'S LIKE DET WAS SAYIN', YE'VE BEEN IN STRANGE FORM SINCE YE GOT BACK.
AYE, WELL... IT CAN BE A BIT FRUSTRATIN' SOMETIMES... BUT...
AYE, BUT YE NEVER KEN, DO YE?
YE CAN KEEP THE PHOTIE THERE, BY THE WAY.
AW, CHEERS!

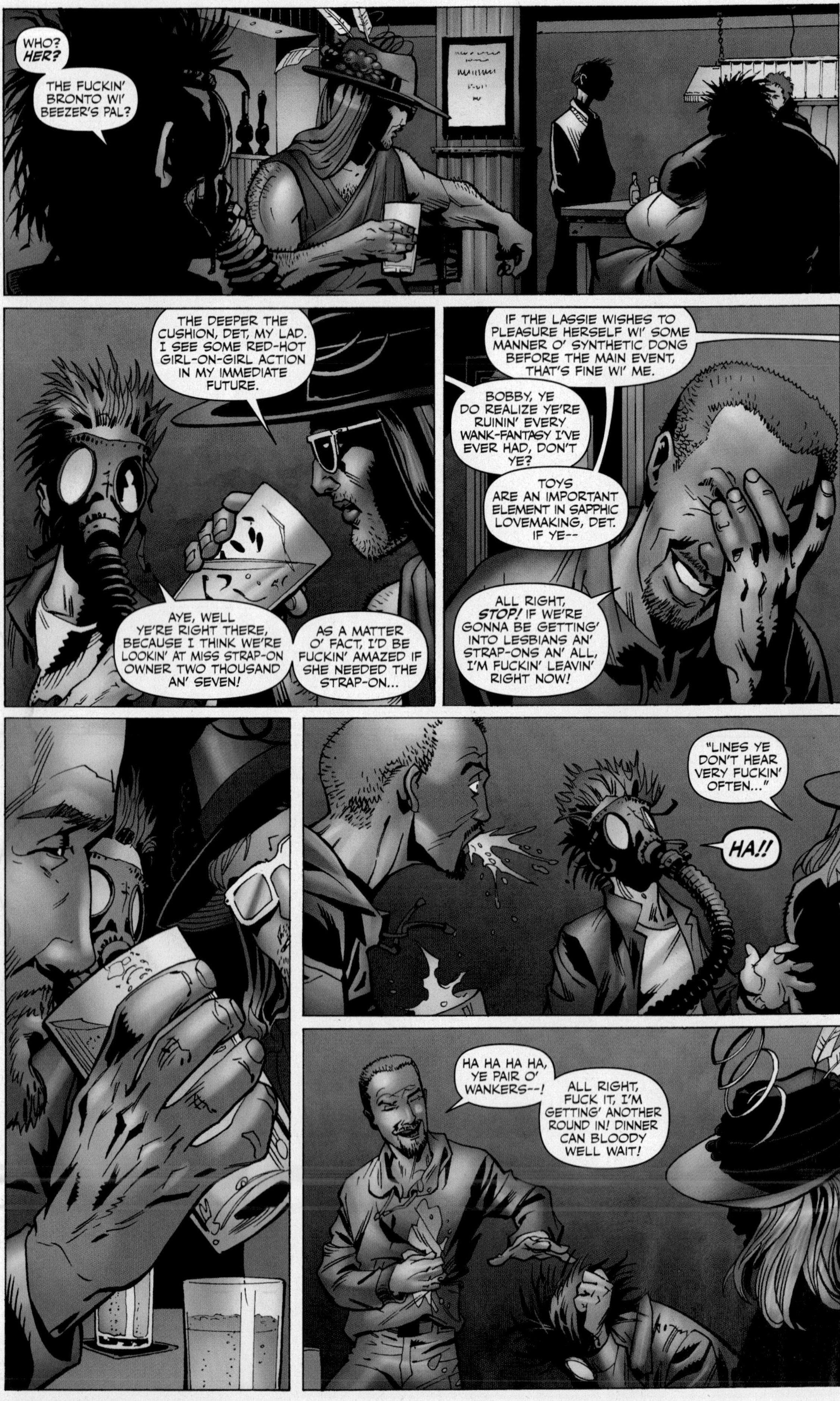
WHO? HER?
THE FUCKIN' BRONTO WI' BEEZER'S PAL?
THE DEEPER THE CUSHION, DET, MY LAD. I SEE SOME RED-HOT GIRL-ON-GIRL ACTION IN MY IMMEDIATE FUTURE.
AYE, WELL YE'RE RIGHT THERE, BECAUSE I THINK WE'RE LOOKIN' AT MISS STRAP-ON OWNER TWO THOUSAND AN' SEVEN!
AS A MATTER O' FACT, I'D BE FUCKIN' AMAZED IF SHE NEEDED THE STRAP-ON...
IF THE LASSIE WISHES TO PLEASURE HERSELF WI' SOME MANNER O' SYNTHETIC DONG BEFORE THE MAIN EVENT, THAT'S FINE WI' ME.
BOBBY, YE DO REALIZE YE'RE RUININ' EVERY WANK-FANTASY I'VE EVER HAD, DON'T YE?
TOYS ARE AN IMPORTANT ELEMENT IN SAPPHIC LOVEMAKING, DET. IF YE--
ALL RIGHT, STOP! IF WE'RE GONNA BE GETTING' INTO LESBIANS AN' STRAP-ONS AN' ALL, I'M FUCKIN' LEAVIN' RIGHT NOW!
"LINES YE DON'T HEAR VERY FUCKIN' OFTEN..."
HA!!
HA HA HA HA, YE PAIR O' WANKERS--!
ALL RIGHT, FUCK IT, I'M GETTING' ANOTHER ROUND IN! DINNER CAN BLOODY WELL WAIT!

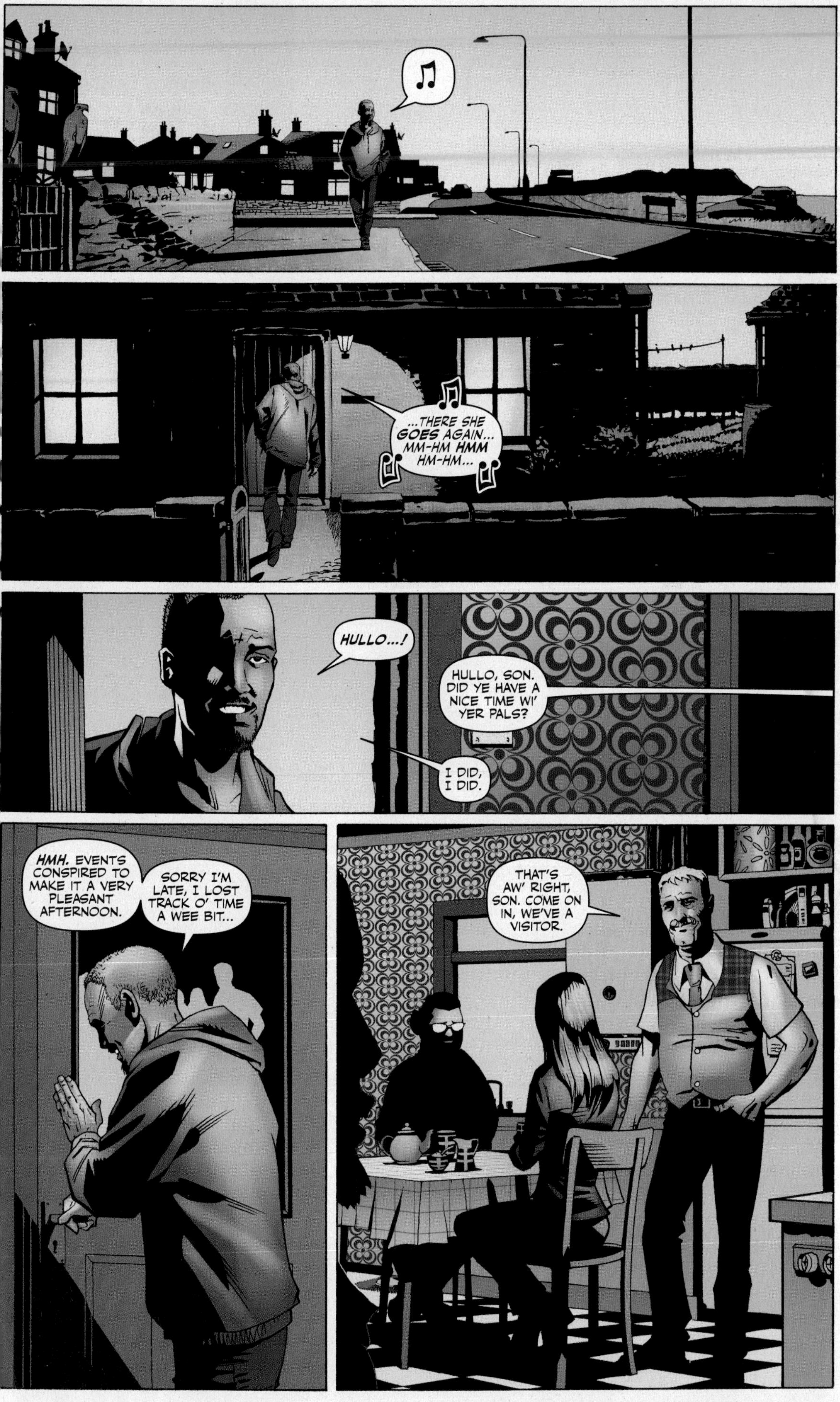
♫
...THERE SHE GOES AGAIN... MM-HM HMM HM-HM...
HULLO...!
HULLO, SON. DID YE HAVE A NICE TIME WI' YER PALS?
I DID, I DID.
HMH. EVENTS CONSPIRED TO MAKE IT A VERY PLEASANT AFTERNOON.
SORRY I'M LATE, I LOST TRACK O' TIME A WEE BIT...
THAT'S AW' RIGHT, SON. COME ON IN, WE'VE A VISITOR.

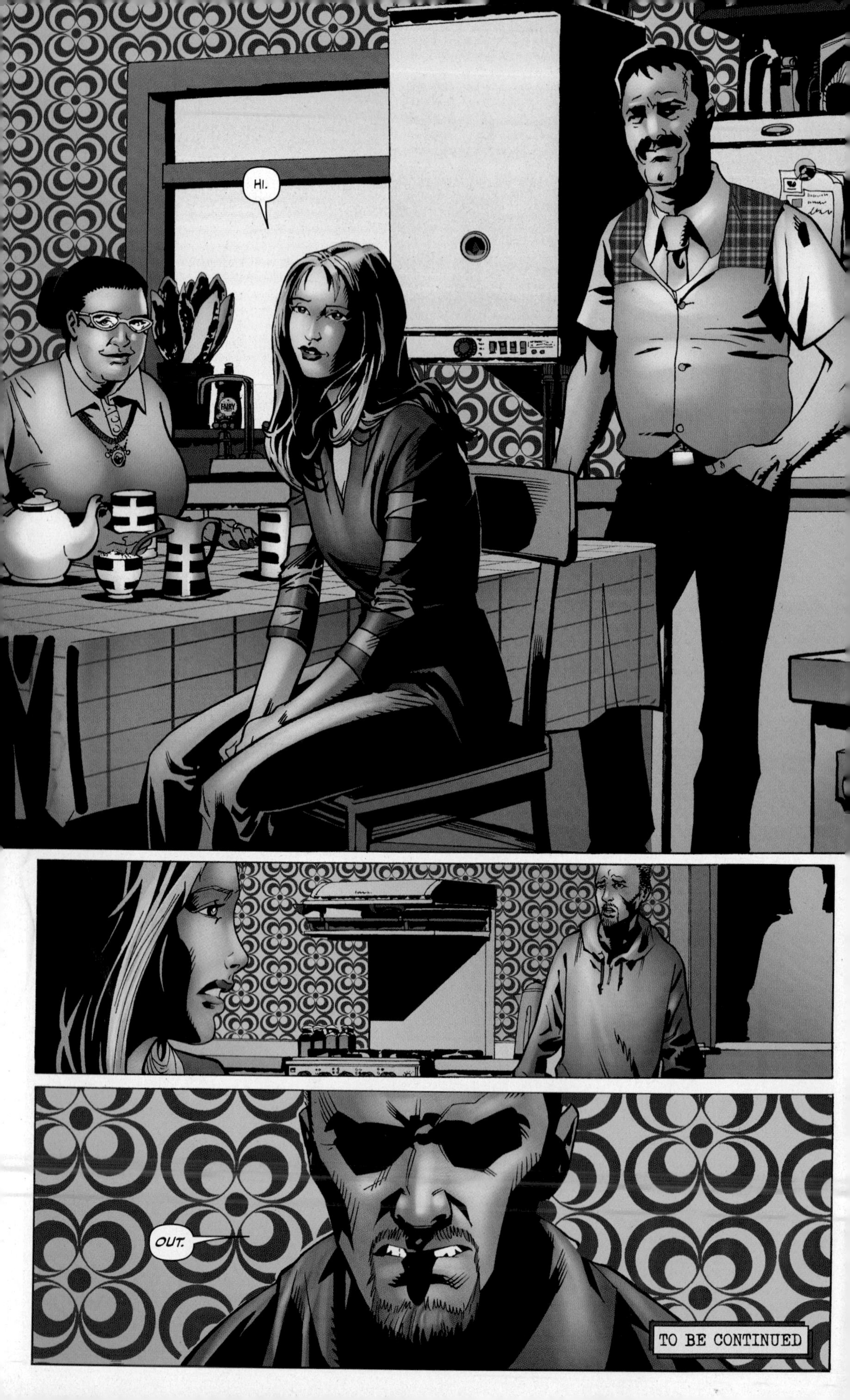
HI.
OUT.
TO BE CONTINUED

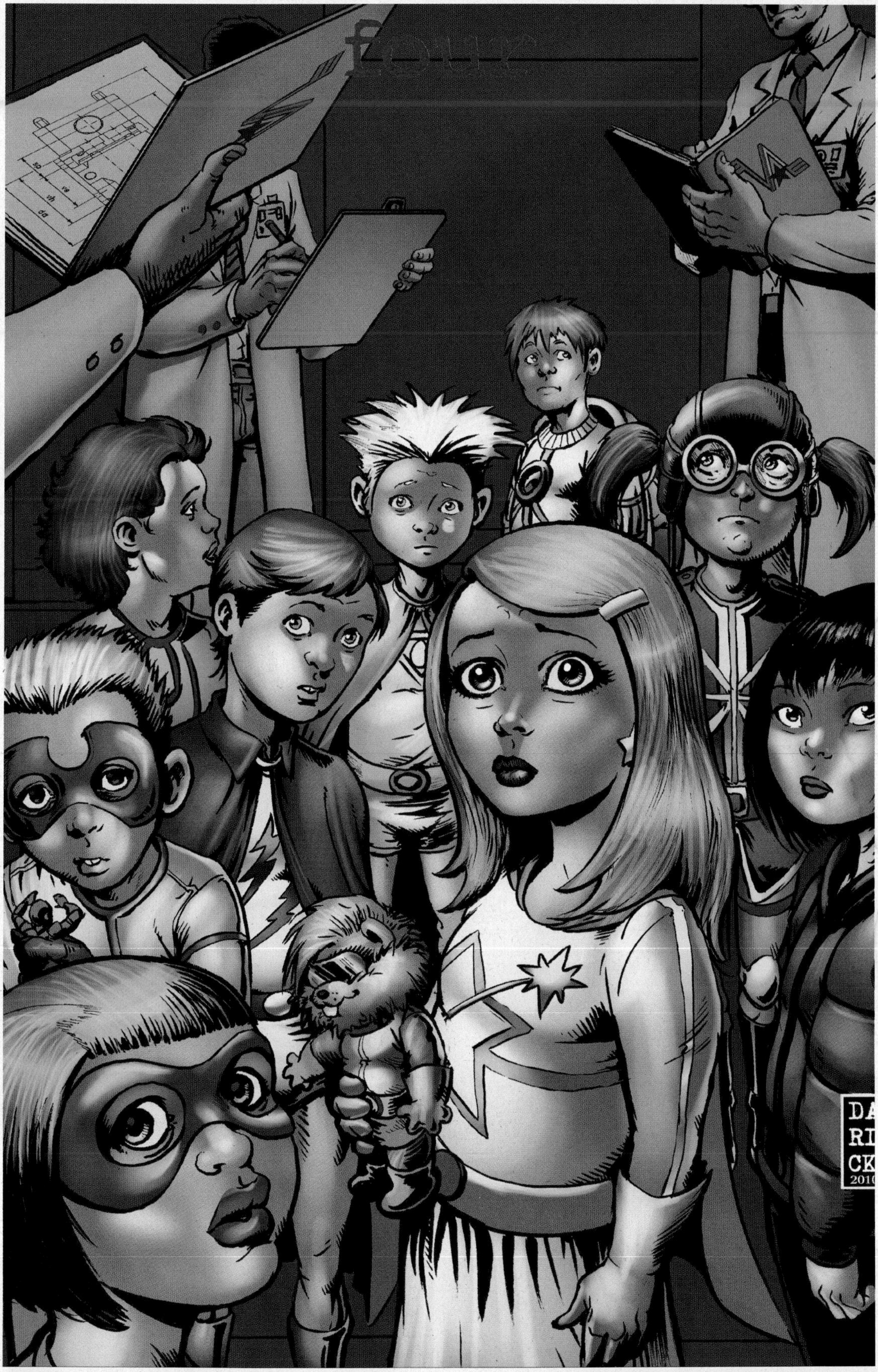

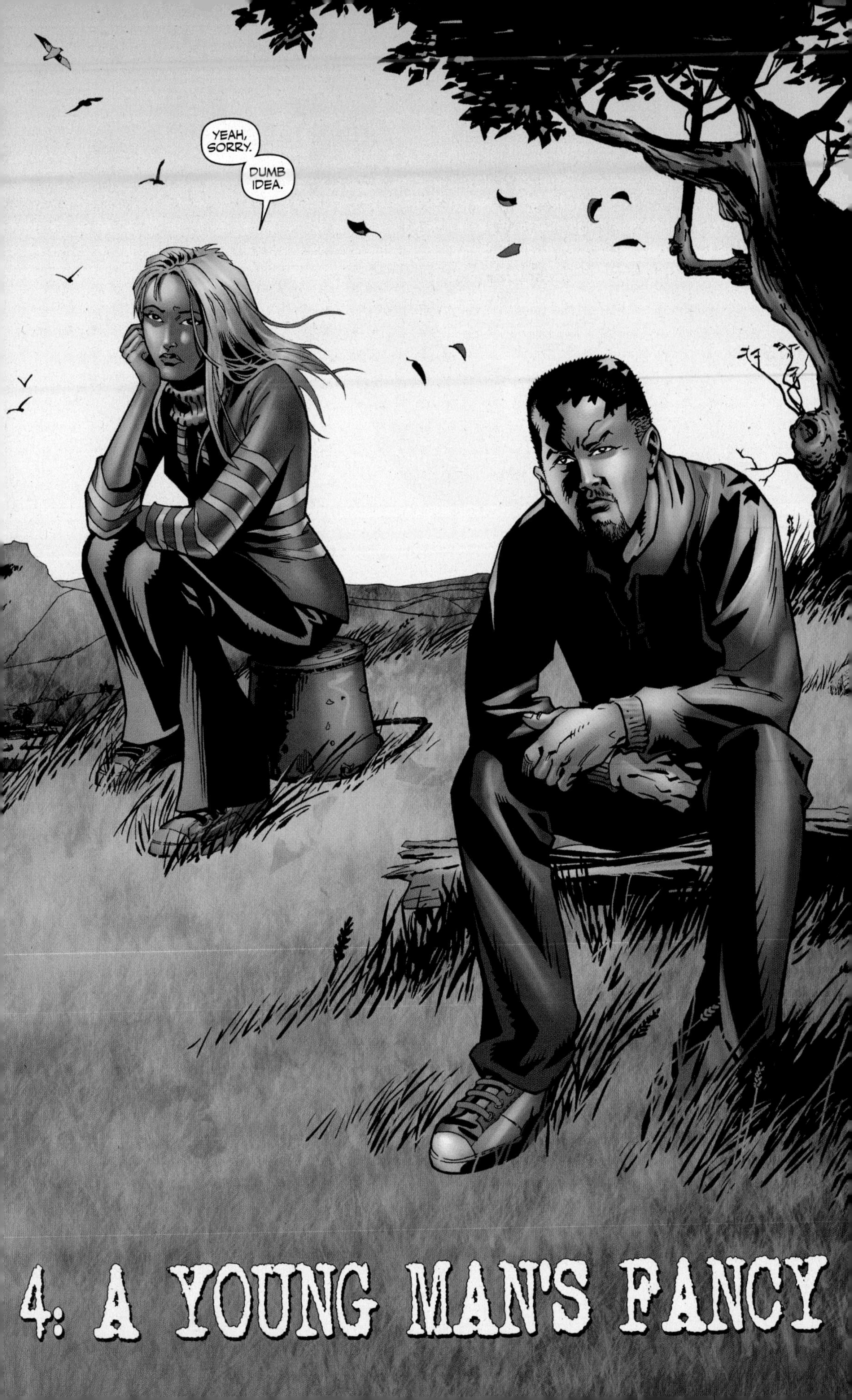

YEAH, SORRY.
DUMB IDEA.
4: A YOUNG MAN'S FANCY

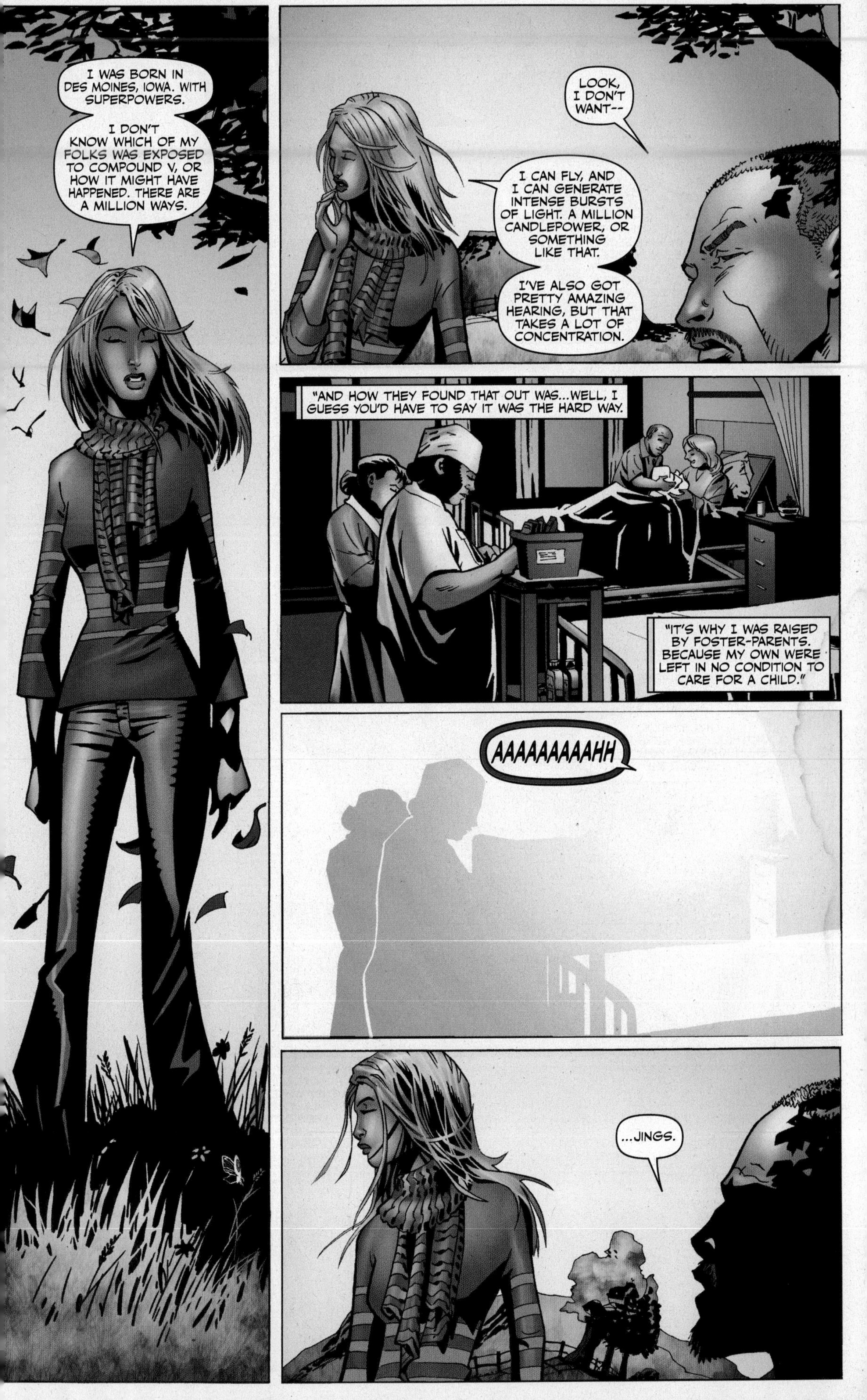
I WAS BORN IN DES MOINES, IOWA. WITH SUPERPOWERS.
I DON'T KNOW WHICH OF MY FOLKS WAS EXPOSED TO COMPOUND V, OR HOW IT MIGHT HAVE HAPPENED. THERE ARE A MILLION WAYS.
LOOK, I DON'T WANT--
I CAN FLY, AND I CAN GENERATE INTENSE BURSTS OF LIGHT. A MILLION CANDLEPOWER, OR SOMETHING LIKE THAT.
I'VE ALSO GOT PRETTY AMAZING HEARING, BUT THAT TAKES A LOT OF CONCENTRATION.
"AND HOW THEY FOUND THAT OUT WAS...WELL, I GUESS YOU'D HAVE TO SAY IT WAS THE HARD WAY.
"IT'S WHY I WAS RAISED BY FOSTER-PARENTS. BECAUSE MY OWN WERE LEFT IN NO CONDITION TO CARE FOR A CHILD."
AAAAAAAAAHH
...JINGS.

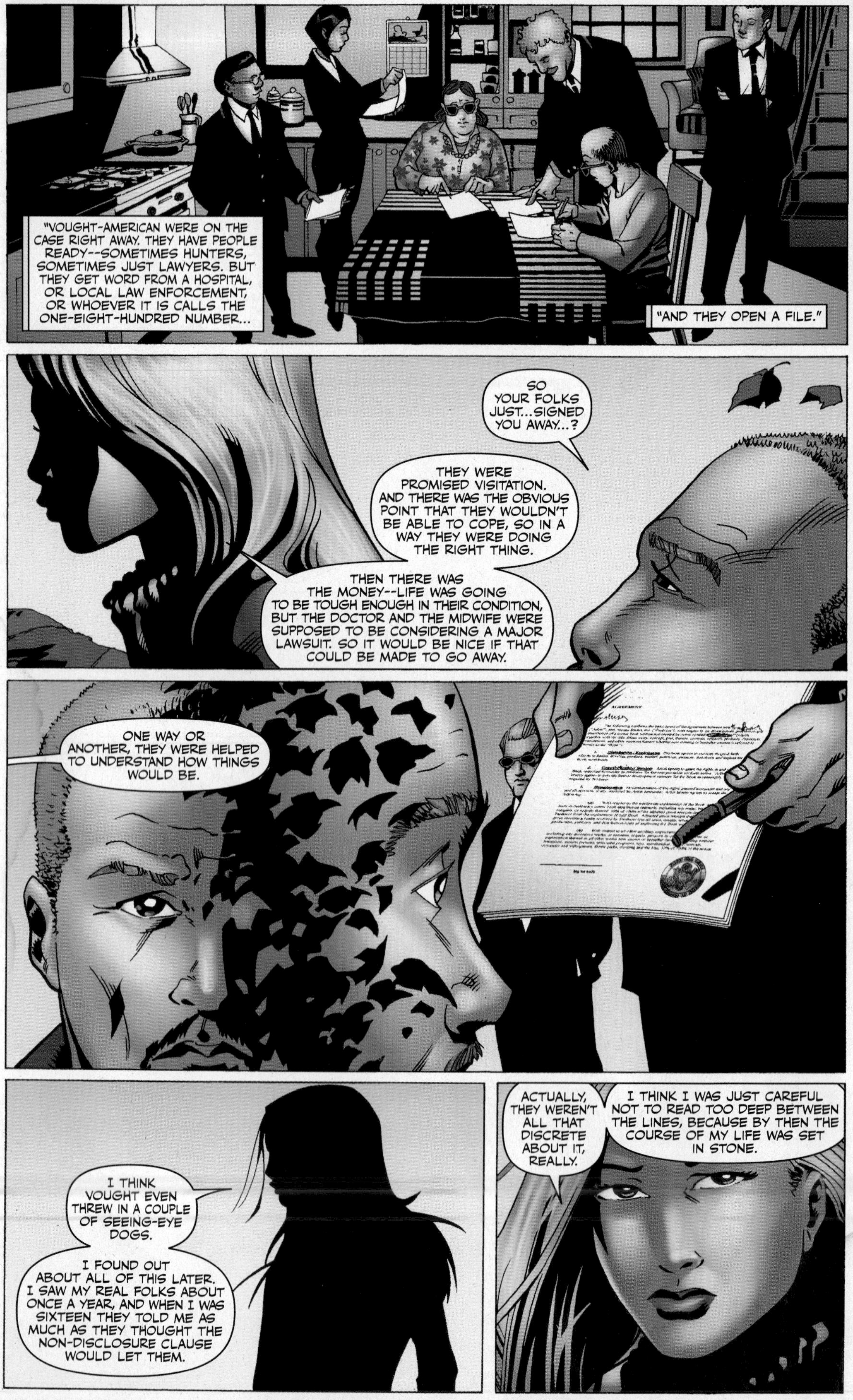
"VOUGHT-AMERICAN WERE ON THE CASE RIGHT AWAY. THEY HAVE PEOPLE READY--SOMETIMES HUNTERS, SOMETIMES JUST LAWYERS. BUT THEY GET WORD FROM A HOSPITAL, OR LOCAL LAW ENFORCEMENT, OR WHOEVER IT IS CALLS THE ONE-EIGHT-HUNDRED NUMBER...
"AND THEY OPEN A FILE."
SO YOUR FOLKS JUST...SIGNED YOU AWAY...?
THEY WERE PROMISED VISITATION. AND THERE WAS THE OBVIOUS POINT THAT THEY WOULDN'T BE ABLE TO COPE, SO IN A WAY THEY WERE DOING THE RIGHT THING.
THEN THERE WAS THE MONEY--LIFE WAS GOING TO BE TOUGH ENOUGH IN THEIR CONDITION, BUT THE DOCTOR AND THE MIDWIFE WERE SUPPOSED TO BE CONSIDERING A MAJOR LAWSUIT. SO IT WOULD BE NICE IF THAT COULD BE MADE TO GO AWAY.
ONE WAY OR ANOTHER, THEY WERE HELPED TO UNDERSTAND HOW THINGS WOULD BE.
I THINK VOUGHT EVEN THREW IN A COUPLE OF SEEING-EYE DOGS.
I FOUND OUT ABOUT ALL OF THIS LATER. I SAW MY REAL FOLKS ABOUT ONCE A YEAR, AND WHEN I WAS SIXTEEN THEY TOLD ME AS MUCH AS THEY THOUGHT THE NON-DISCLOSURE CLAUSE WOULD LET THEM.
ACTUALLY, THEY WEREN'T ALL THAT DISCRETE ABOUT IT, REALLY.
I THINK I WAS JUST CAREFUL NOT TO READ TOO DEEP BETWEEN THE LINES, BECAUSE BY THEN THE COURSE OF MY LIFE WAS SET IN STONE.

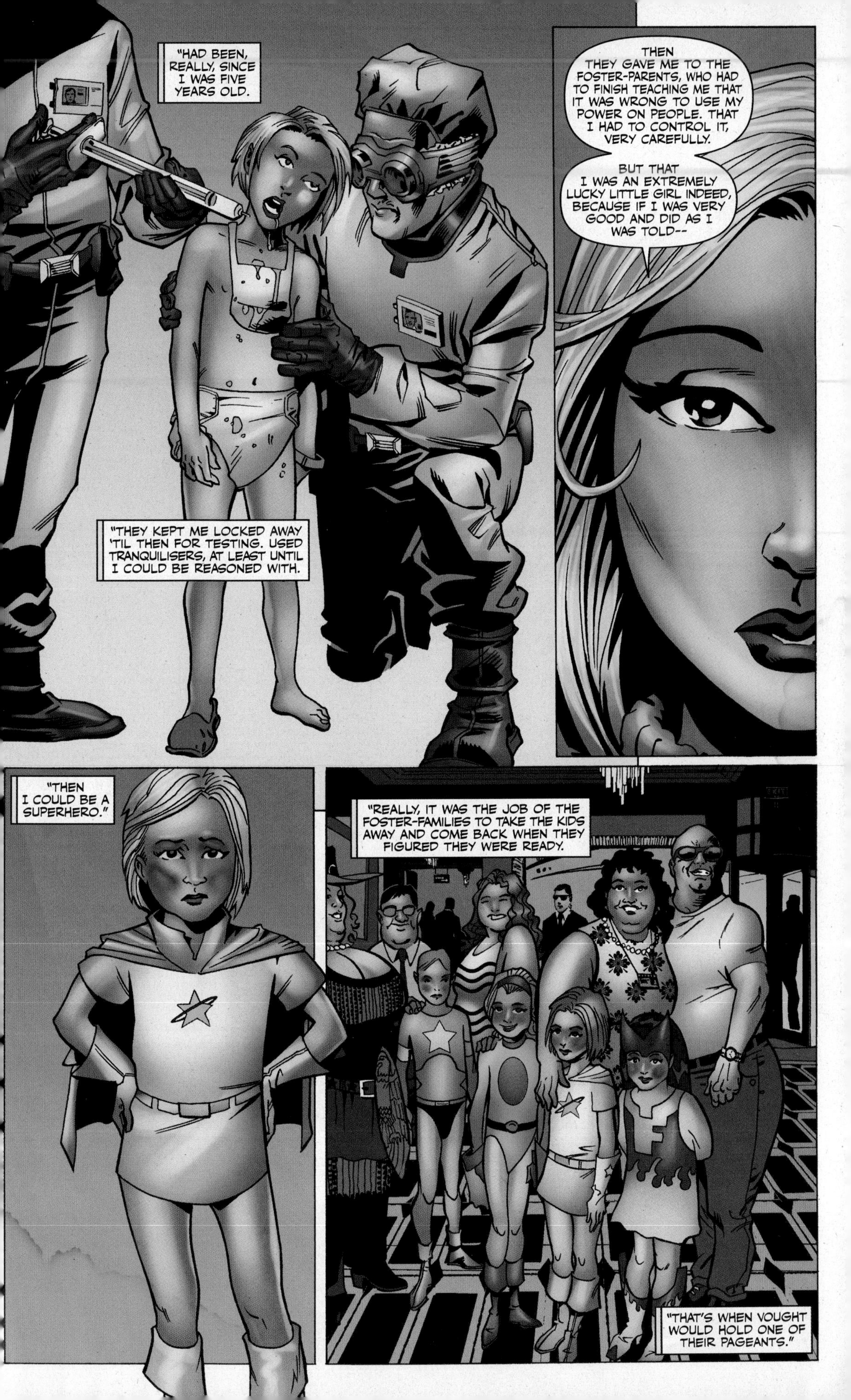
"HAD BEEN, REALLY, SINCE I WAS FIVE YEARS OLD.
"THEY KEPT ME LOCKED AWAY 'TIL THEN FOR TESTING. USED TRANQUILISERS, AT LEAST UNTIL I COULD BE REASONED WITH.
THEN THEY GAVE ME TO THE FOSTER-PARENTS, WHO HAD TO FINISH TEACHING ME THAT IT WAS WRONG TO USE MY POWER ON PEOPLE. THAT I HAD TO CONTROL IT, VERY CAREFULLY.
BUT THAT I WAS AN EXTREMELY LUCKY LITTLE GIRL INDEED, BECAUSE IF I WAS VERY GOOD AND DID AS I WAS TOLD--
"THEN I COULD BE A SUPERHERO."
"REALLY, IT WAS THE JOB OF THE FOSTER-FAMILIES TO TAKE THE KIDS AWAY AND COME BACK WHEN THEY FIGURED THEY WERE READY.
"THAT'S WHEN VOUGHT WOULD HOLD ONE OF THEIR PAGEANTS."

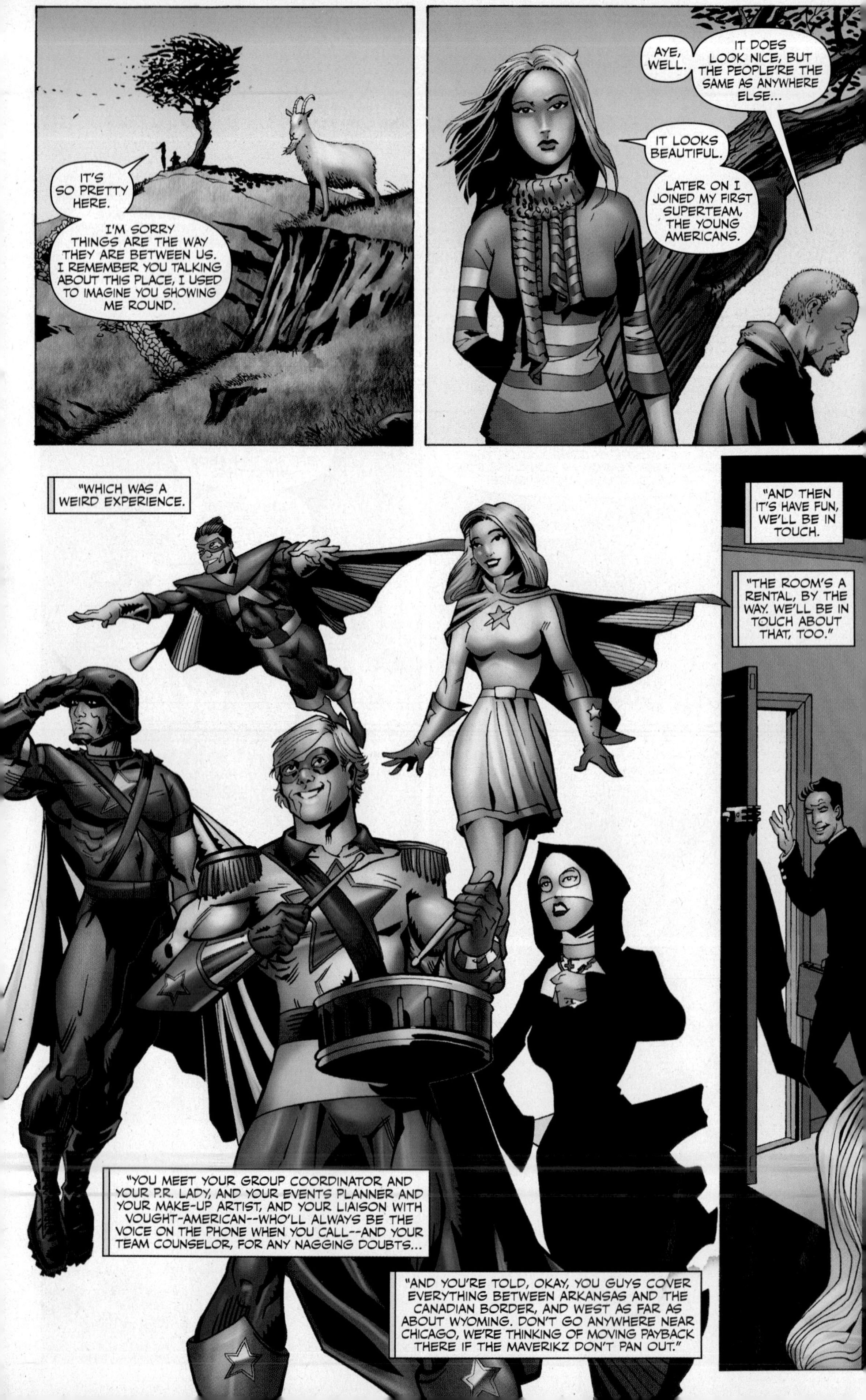
IT'S SO PRETTY HERE.
I'M SORRY THINGS ARE THE WAY THEY ARE BETWEEN US. I REMEMBER YOU TALKING ABOUT THIS PLACE, I USED TO IMAGINE YOU SHOWING ME ROUND.
AYE, WELL.
IT DOES LOOK NICE, BUT THE PEOPLE'RE THE SAME AS ANYWHERE ELSE...
IT LOOKS BEAUTIFUL.
LATER ON I JOINED MY FIRST SUPERTEAM, THE YOUNG AMERICANS.
"WHICH WAS A WEIRD EXPERIENCE.
"YOU MEET YOUR GROUP COORDINATOR AND YOUR P.R. LADY, AND YOUR EVENTS PLANNER AND YOUR MAKE-UP ARTIST, AND YOUR LIAISON WITH VOUGHT-AMERICAN--WHO'LL ALWAYS BE THE VOICE ON THE PHONE WHEN YOU CALL--AND YOUR TEAM COUNSELOR, FOR ANY NAGGING DOUBTS...
"AND YOU'RE TOLD, OKAY, YOU GUYS COVER EVERYTHING BETWEEN ARKANSAS AND THE CANADIAN BORDER, AND WEST AS FAR AS ABOUT WYOMING. DON'T GO ANYWHERE NEAR CHICAGO, WE'RE THINKING OF MOVING PAYBACK THERE IF THE MAVERIKZ DON'T PAN OUT."
"AND THEN IT'S HAVE FUN, WE'LL BE IN TOUCH.
"THE ROOM'S A RENTAL, BY THE WAY. WE'LL BE IN TOUCH ABOUT THAT, TOO."

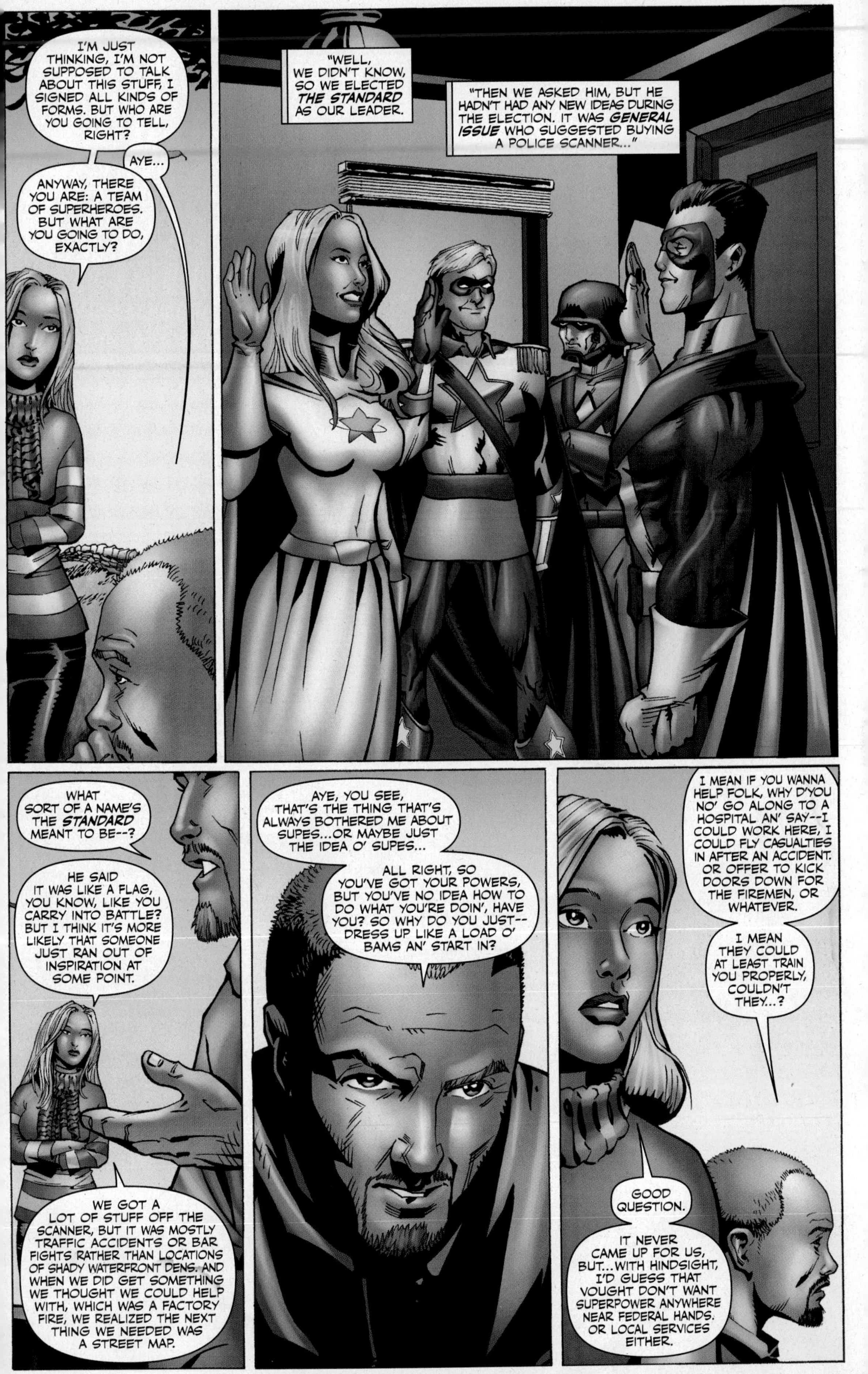
I'M JUST THINKING, I'M NOT SUPPOSED TO TALK ABOUT THIS STUFF, I SIGNED ALL KINDS OF FORMS. BUT WHO ARE YOU GOING TO TELL, RIGHT?
AYE...
ANYWAY, THERE YOU ARE: A TEAM OF SUPERHEROES. BUT WHAT ARE YOU GOING TO DO, EXACTLY?
"WELL, WE DIDN'T KNOW, SO WE ELECTED THE STANDARD AS OUR LEADER.
"THEN WE ASKED HIM, BUT HE HADN'T HAD ANY NEW IDEAS DURING THE ELECTION. IT WAS GENERAL ISSUE WHO SUGGESTED BUYING A POLICE SCANNER..."
WHAT SORT OF A NAME'S THE STANDARD MEANT TO BE--?
HE SAID IT WAS LIKE A FLAG, YOU KNOW, LIKE YOU CARRY INTO BATTLE? BUT I THINK IT'S MORE LIKELY THAT SOMEONE JUST RAN OUT OF INSPIRATION AT SOME POINT.
WE GOT A LOT OF STUFF OFF THE SCANNER, BUT IT WAS MOSTLY TRAFFIC ACCIDENTS OR BAR FIGHTS RATHER THAN LOCATIONS OF SHADY WATERFRONT DENS. AND WHEN WE DID GET SOMETHING WE THOUGHT WE COULD HELP WITH, WHICH WAS A FACTORY FIRE, WE REALIZED THE NEXT THING WE NEEDED WAS A STREET MAP.
AYE, YOU SEE, THAT'S THE THING THAT'S ALWAYS BOTHERED ME ABOUT SUPES...OR MAYBE JUST THE IDEA O' SUPES...
ALL RIGHT, SO YOU'VE GOT YOUR POWERS, BUT YOU'VE NO IDEA HOW TO DO WHAT YOU'RE DOIN', HAVE YOU? SO WHY DO YOU JUST-- DRESS UP LIKE A LOAD O' BAMS AN' START IN?
I MEAN IF YOU WANNA HELP FOLK, WHY D'YOU NO' GO ALONG TO A HOSPITAL AN' SAY--I COULD WORK HERE, I COULD FLY CASUALTIES IN AFTER AN ACCIDENT. OR OFFER TO KICK DOORS DOWN FOR THE FIREMEN, OR WHATEVER.
I MEAN THEY COULD AT LEAST TRAIN YOU PROPERLY, COULDN'T THEY...?
GOOD QUESTION.
IT NEVER CAME UP FOR US, BUT...WITH HINDSIGHT, I'D GUESS THAT VOUGHT DON'T WANT SUPERPOWER ANYWHERE NEAR FEDERAL HANDS. OR LOCAL SERVICES EITHER.

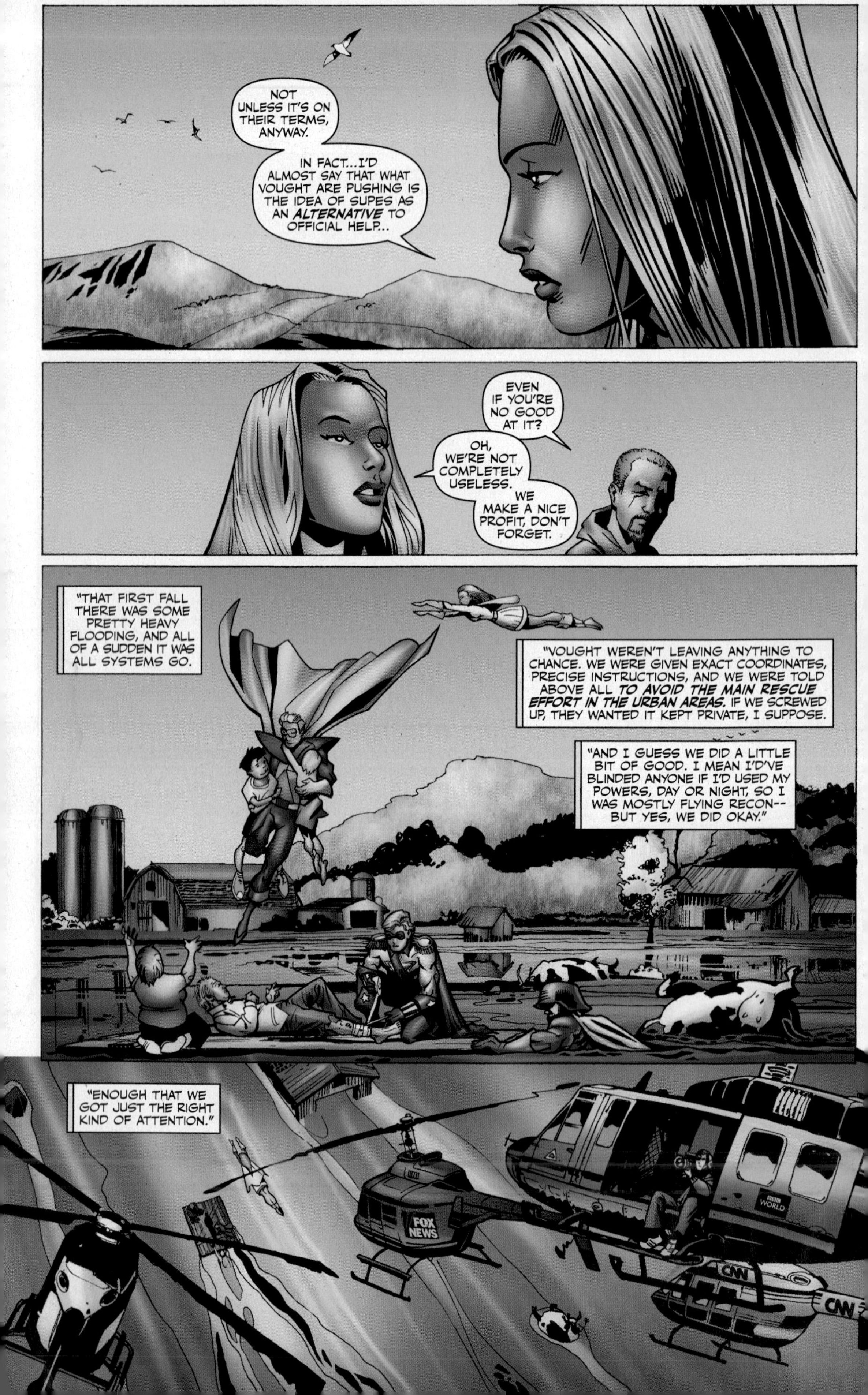
NOT UNLESS IT'S ON THEIR TERMS, ANYWAY.
IN FACT...I'D ALMOST SAY THAT WHAT VOUGHT ARE PUSHING IS THE IDEA OF SUPES AS AN *ALTERNATIVE* TO OFFICIAL HELP...
EVEN IF YOU'RE NO GOOD AT IT?
OH, WE'RE NOT COMPLETELY USELESS.
WE MAKE A NICE PROFIT, DON'T FORGET.
"THAT FIRST FALL THERE WAS SOME PRETTY HEAVY FLOODING, AND ALL OF A SUDDEN IT WAS ALL SYSTEMS GO.
"VOUGHT WEREN'T LEAVING ANYTHING TO CHANCE. WE WERE GIVEN EXACT COORDINATES, PRECISE INSTRUCTIONS, AND WE WERE TOLD ABOVE ALL ***TO AVOID THE MAIN RESCUE EFFORT IN THE URBAN AREAS.*** IF WE SCREWED UP, THEY WANTED IT KEPT PRIVATE, I SUPPOSE.
"AND I GUESS WE DID A LITTLE BIT OF GOOD. I MEAN I'D'VE BLINDED ANYONE IF I'D USED MY POWERS, DAY OR NIGHT, SO I WAS MOSTLY FLYING RECON--BUT YES, WE DID OKAY."
"ENOUGH THAT WE GOT JUST THE RIGHT KIND OF ATTENTION."
FOX NEWS
BBC WORLD
CNN
CNN

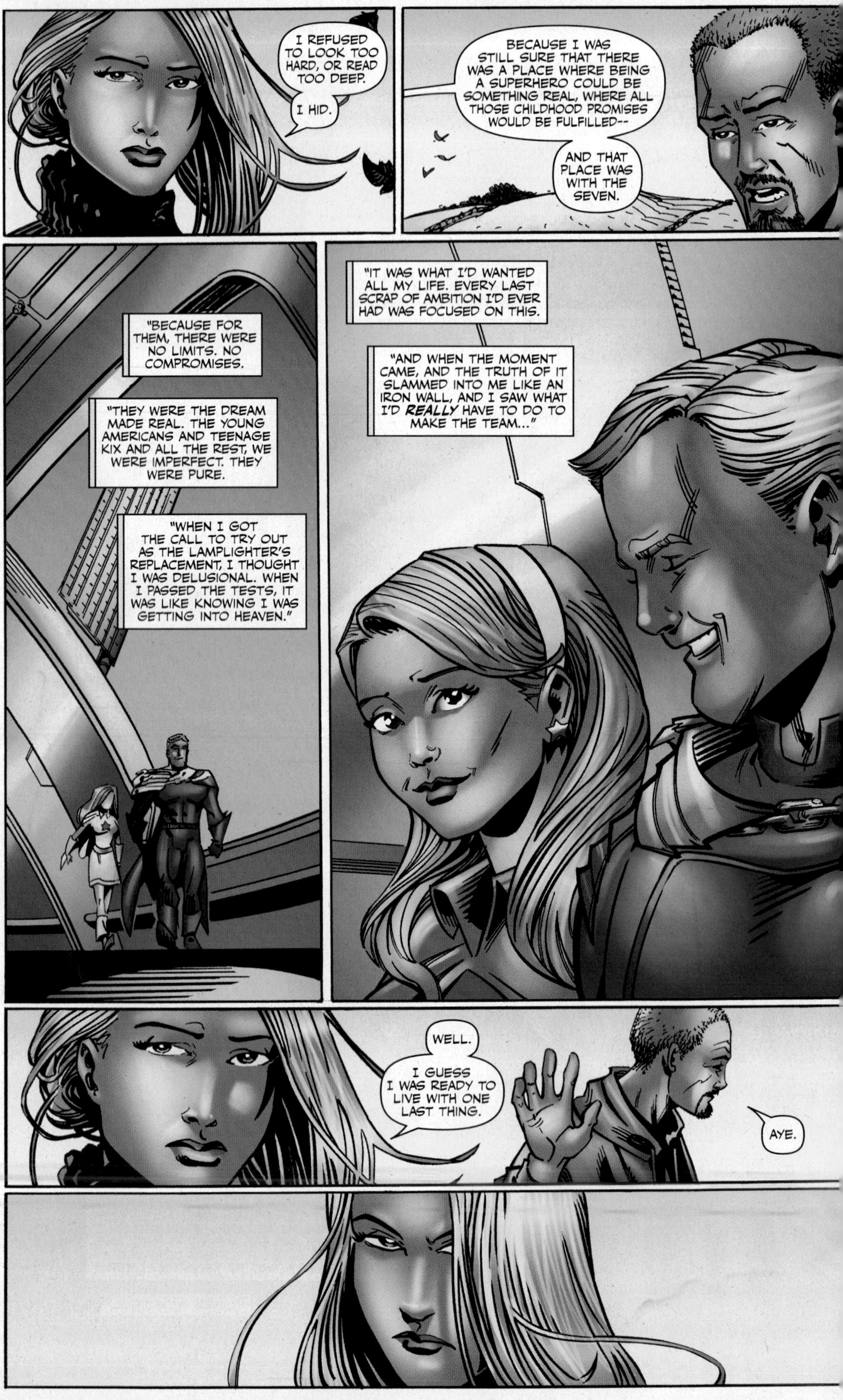

I REFUSED TO LOOK TOO HARD, OR READ TOO DEEP.
I HID.
BECAUSE I WAS STILL SURE THAT THERE WAS A PLACE WHERE BEING A SUPERHERO COULD BE SOMETHING REAL, WHERE ALL THOSE CHILDHOOD PROMISES WOULD BE FULFILLED--
AND THAT PLACE WAS WITH THE SEVEN.
"BECAUSE FOR THEM, THERE WERE NO LIMITS. NO COMPROMISES.
"THEY WERE THE DREAM MADE REAL. THE YOUNG AMERICANS AND TEENAGE KIX AND ALL THE REST, WE WERE IMPERFECT. THEY WERE PURE.
"WHEN I GOT THE CALL TO TRY OUT AS THE LAMPLIGHTER'S REPLACEMENT, I THOUGHT I WAS DELUSIONAL. WHEN I PASSED THE TESTS, IT WAS LIKE KNOWING I WAS GETTING INTO HEAVEN."
"IT WAS WHAT I'D WANTED ALL MY LIFE. EVERY LAST SCRAP OF AMBITION I'D EVER HAD WAS FOCUSED ON THIS.
"AND WHEN THE MOMENT CAME, AND THE TRUTH OF IT SLAMMED INTO ME LIKE AN IRON WALL, AND I SAW WHAT I'D *REALLY* HAVE TO DO TO MAKE THE TEAM..."
WELL.
I GUESS I WAS READY TO LIVE WITH ONE LAST THING.
AYE.

TO BE CONTINUED

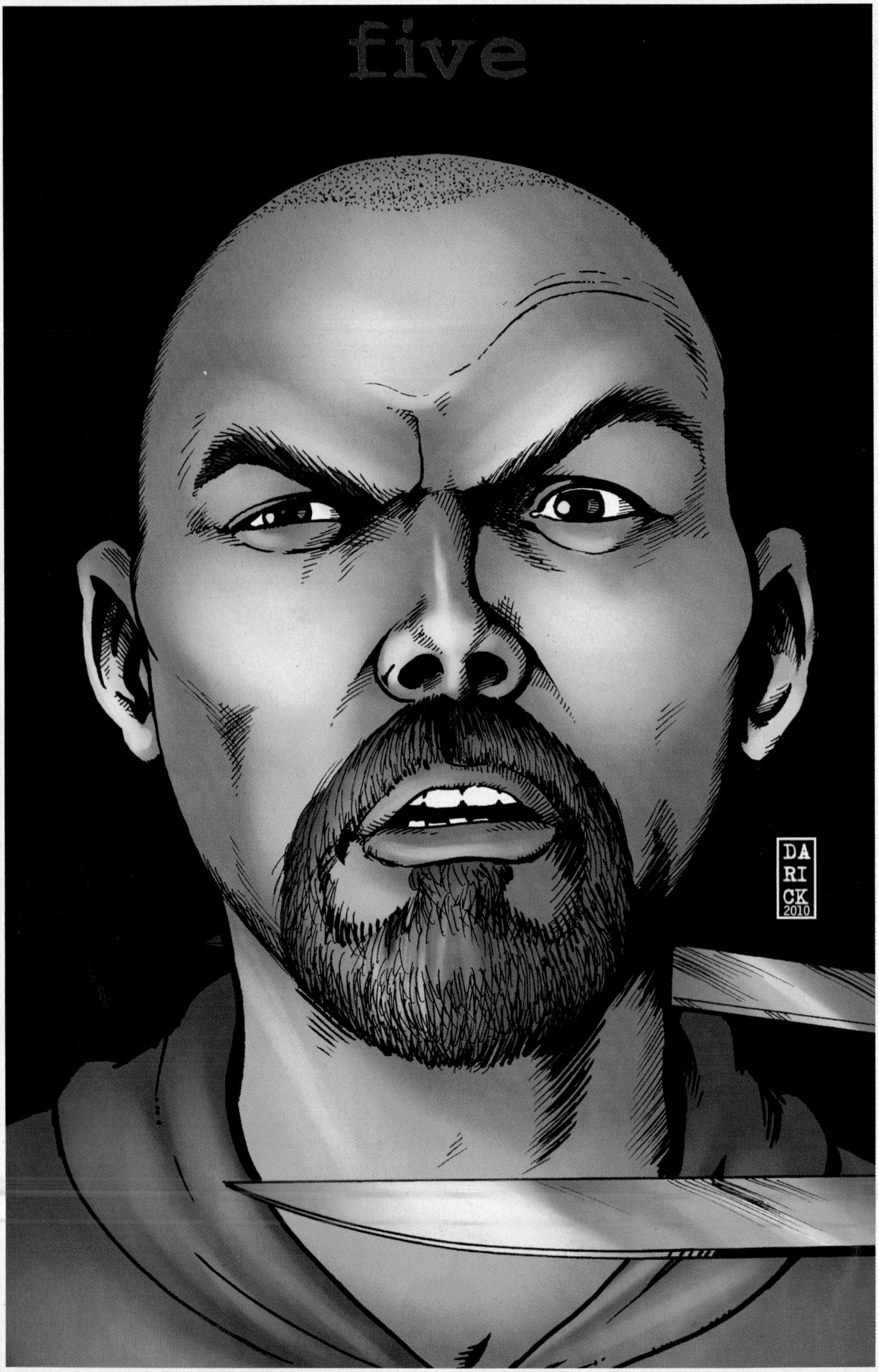
five
DA
RI
CK
2010

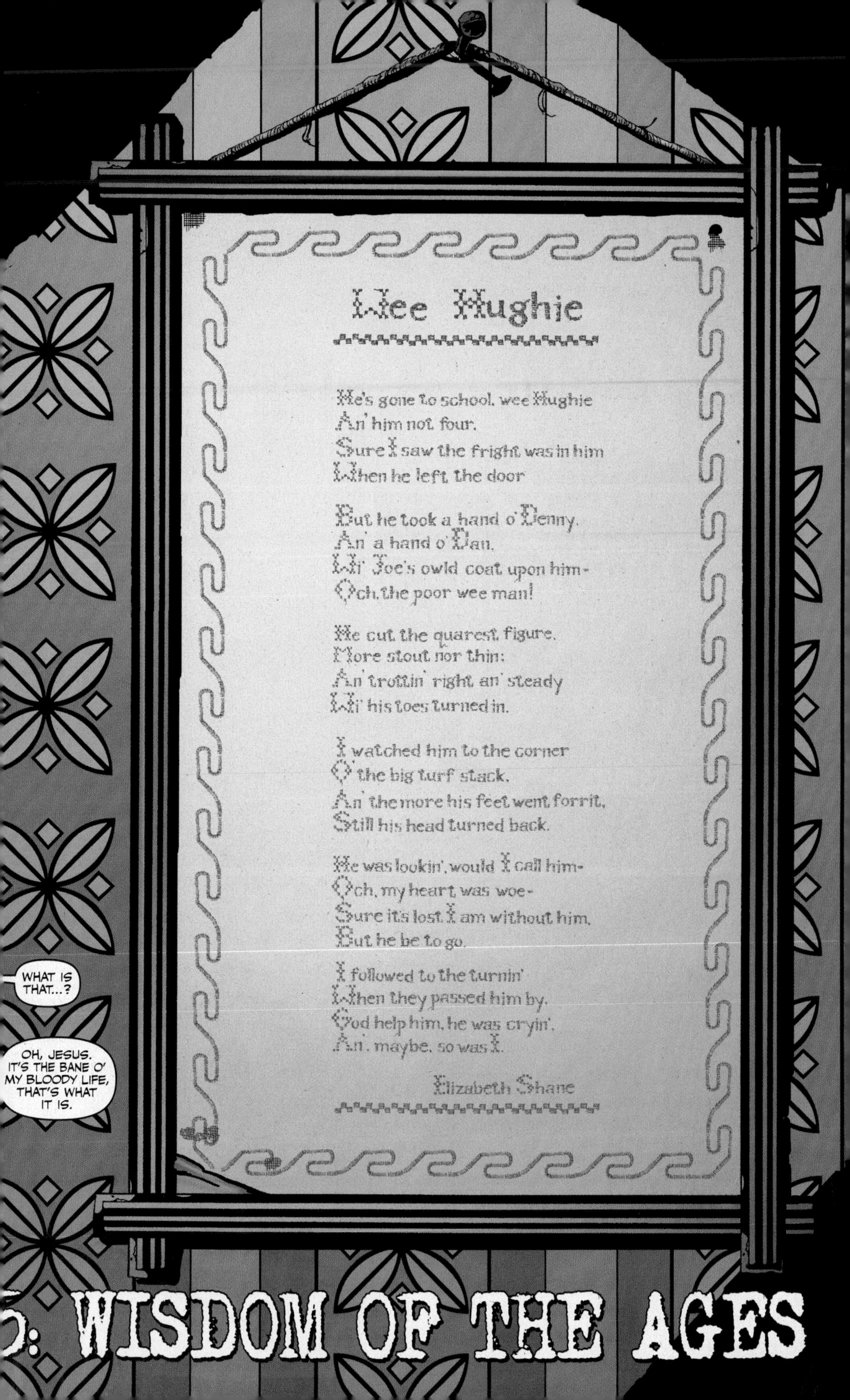
Wee Hughie
He's gone to school, wee Hughie
An' him not four,
Sure I saw the fright was in him
When he left the door
But he took a hand o' Denny,
An' a hand o' Dan,
Wi' Joe's owld coat upon him-
Och, the poor wee man!
He cut the quarest figure,
More stout nor thin;
An' trottin' right an' steady
Wi' his toes turned in.
I watched him to the corner
O' the big turf stack,
An' the more his feet went forrit,
Still his head turned back.
He was lookin', would I call him-
Och, my heart was woe-
Sure it's lost I am without him,
But he be to go.
I followed to the turnin'
When they passed him by,
God help him, he was cryin',
An', maybe, so was I.
Elizabeth Shane
WHAT IS THAT...?
OH, JESUS. IT'S THE BANE O' MY BLOODY LIFE, THAT'S WHAT IT IS.
5: WISDOM OF THE AGES

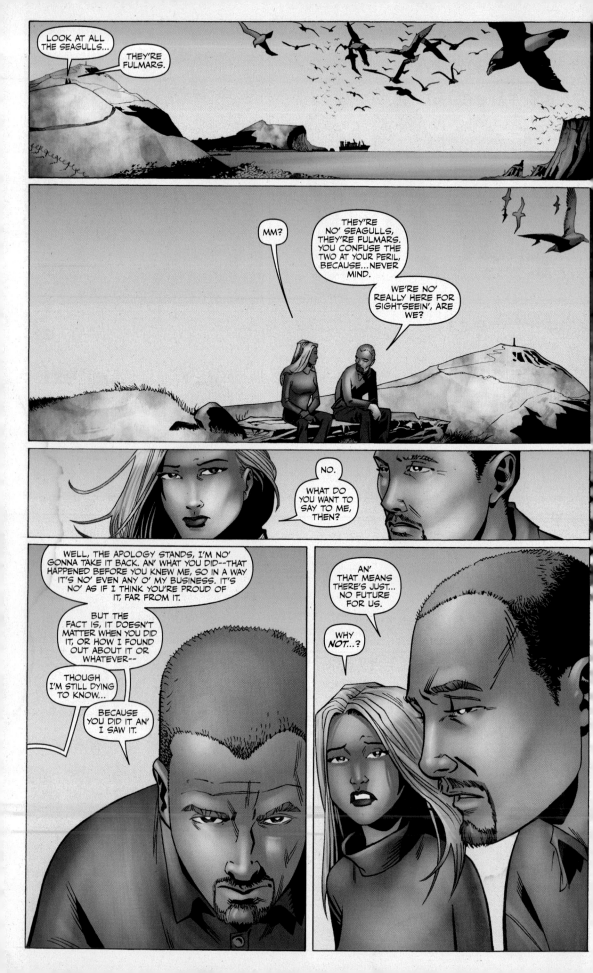

TO BE CONCLUDED

six

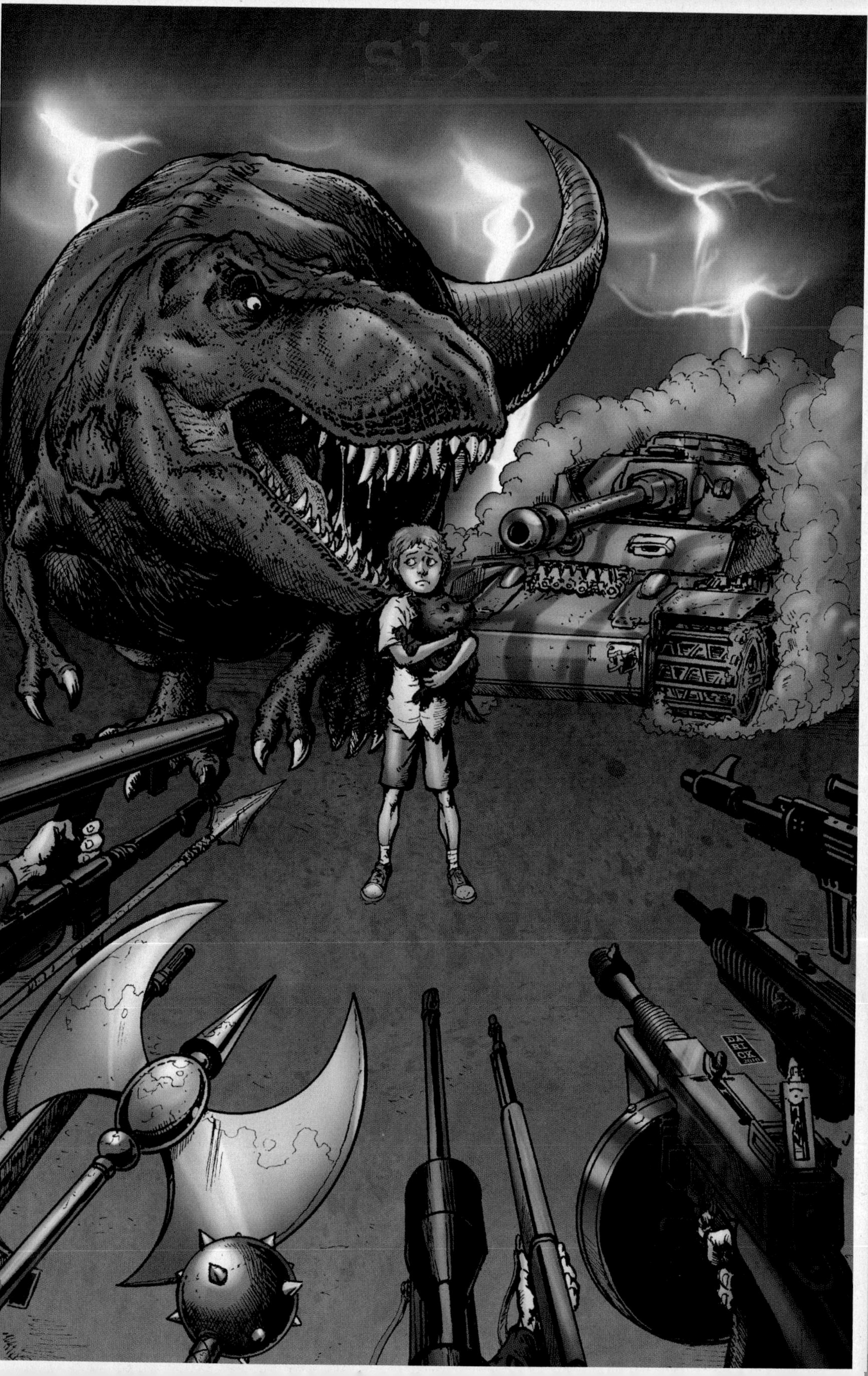

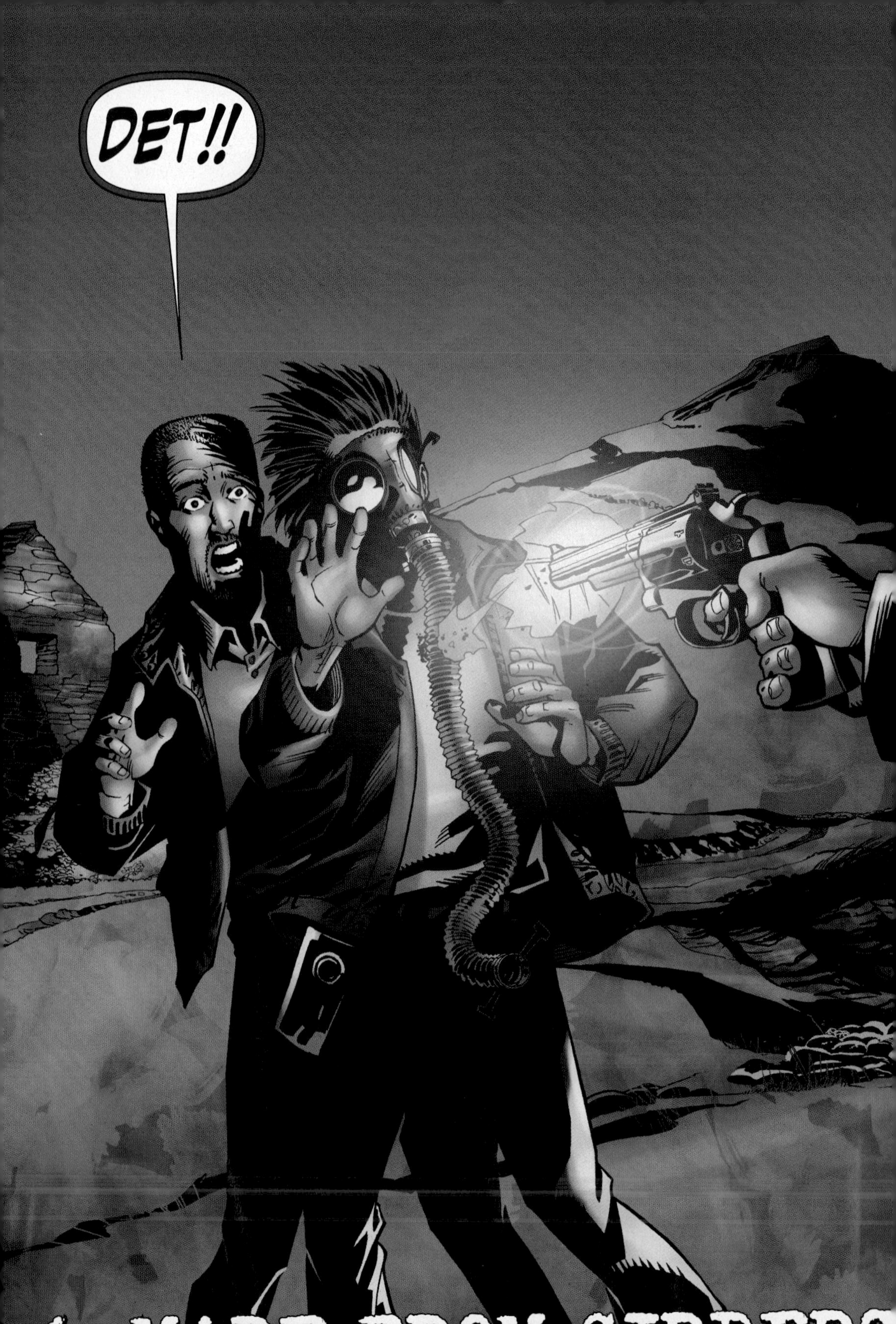
DET!!

6. MADE FROM GIRDERS

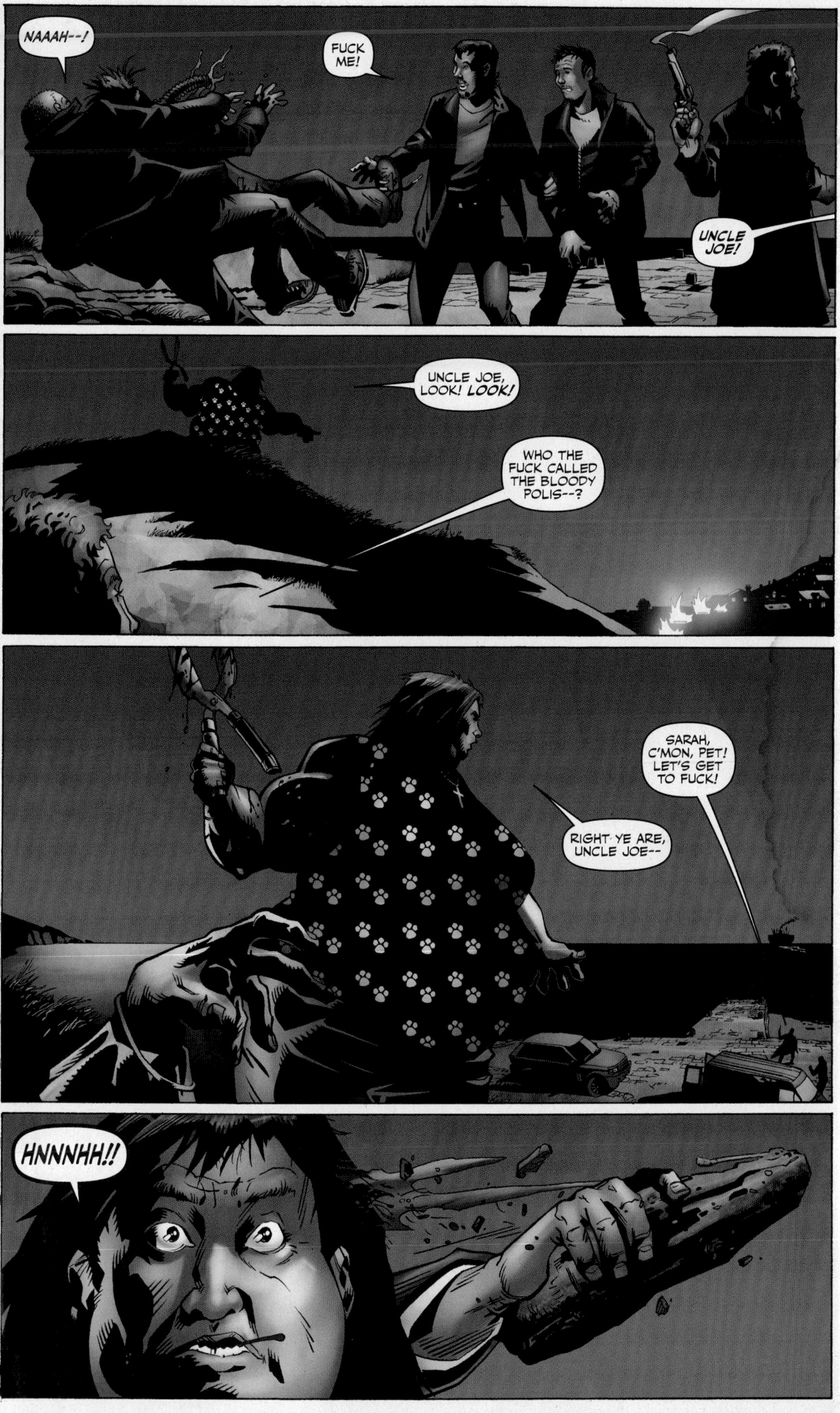
NAAAH--!
FUCK ME!
UNCLE JOE!
UNCLE JOE, LOOK! LOOK!
WHO THE FUCK CALLED THE BLOODY POLIS--?
SARAH, C'MON, PET! LET'S GET TO FUCK!
RIGHT YE ARE, UNCLE JOE--
HNNNHH!!

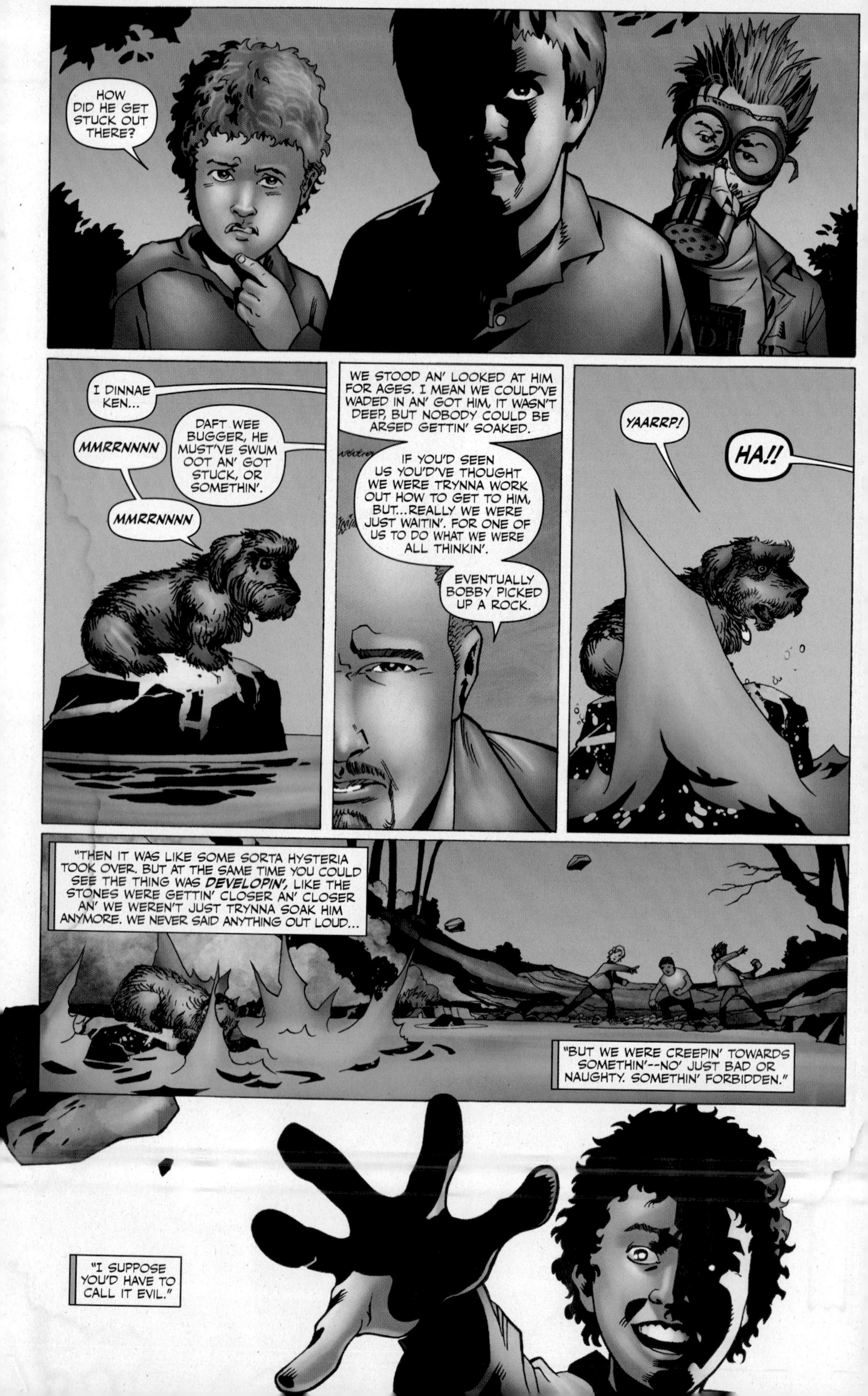

HOW DID HE GET STUCK OUT THERE?
I DINNAE KEN...
MMRRNNNN
DAFT WEE BUGGER, HE MUST'VE SWUM OOT AN' GOT STUCK, OR SOMETHIN'.
MMRRNNNN
WE STOOD AN' LOOKED AT HIM FOR AGES. I MEAN WE COULD'VE WADED IN AN' GOT HIM, IT WASN'T DEEP, BUT NOBODY COULD BE ARSED GETTIN' SOAKED.
IF YOU'D SEEN US YOU'D'VE THOUGHT WE WERE TRYNNA WORK OUT HOW TO GET TO HIM, BUT...REALLY WE WERE JUST WAITIN'. FOR ONE OF US TO DO WHAT WE WERE ALL THINKIN'.
EVENTUALLY BOBBY PICKED UP A ROCK.
YAARRP!
HA!!
"THEN IT WAS LIKE SOME SORTA HYSTERIA TOOK OVER. BUT AT THE SAME TIME YOU COULD SEE THE THING WAS DEVELOPIN', LIKE THE STONES WERE GETTIN' CLOSER AN' CLOSER AN' WE WEREN'T JUST TRYNNA SOAK HIM ANYMORE. WE NEVER SAID ANYTHING OUT LOUD...
"BUT WE WERE CREEPIN' TOWARDS SOMETHIN'--NO' JUST BAD OR NAUGHTY. SOMETHIN' FORBIDDEN."
"I SUPPOSE YOU'D HAVE TO CALL IT EVIL."

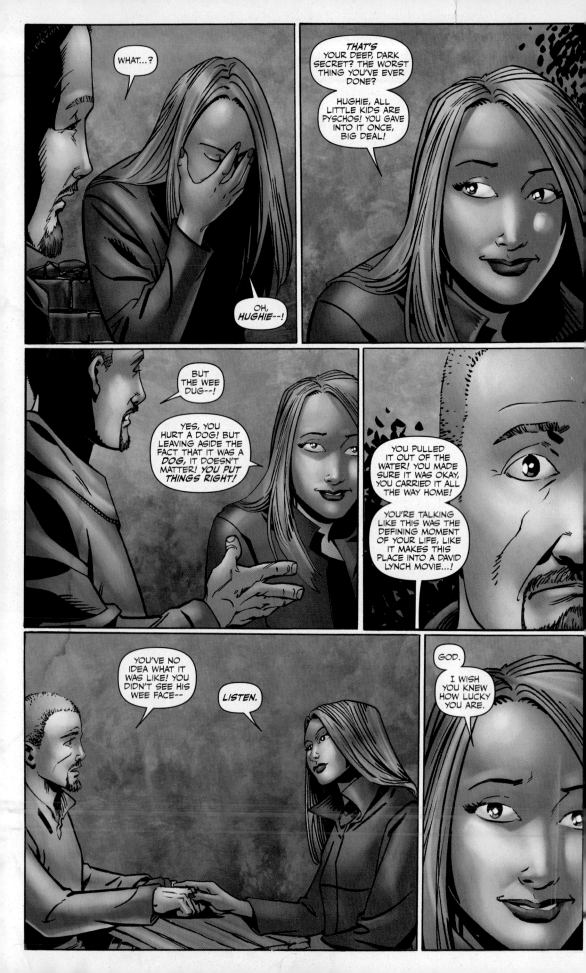

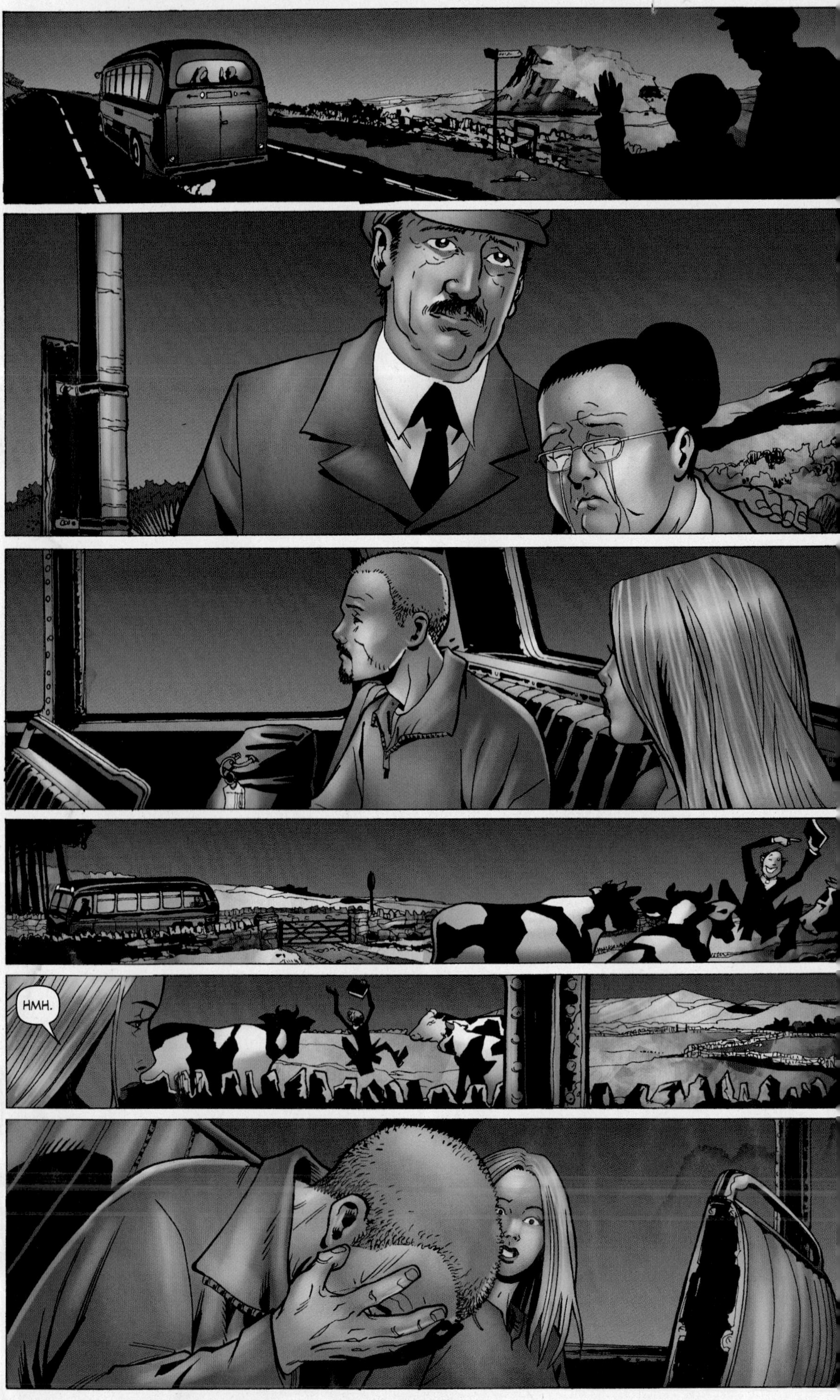
HMH.

THE END

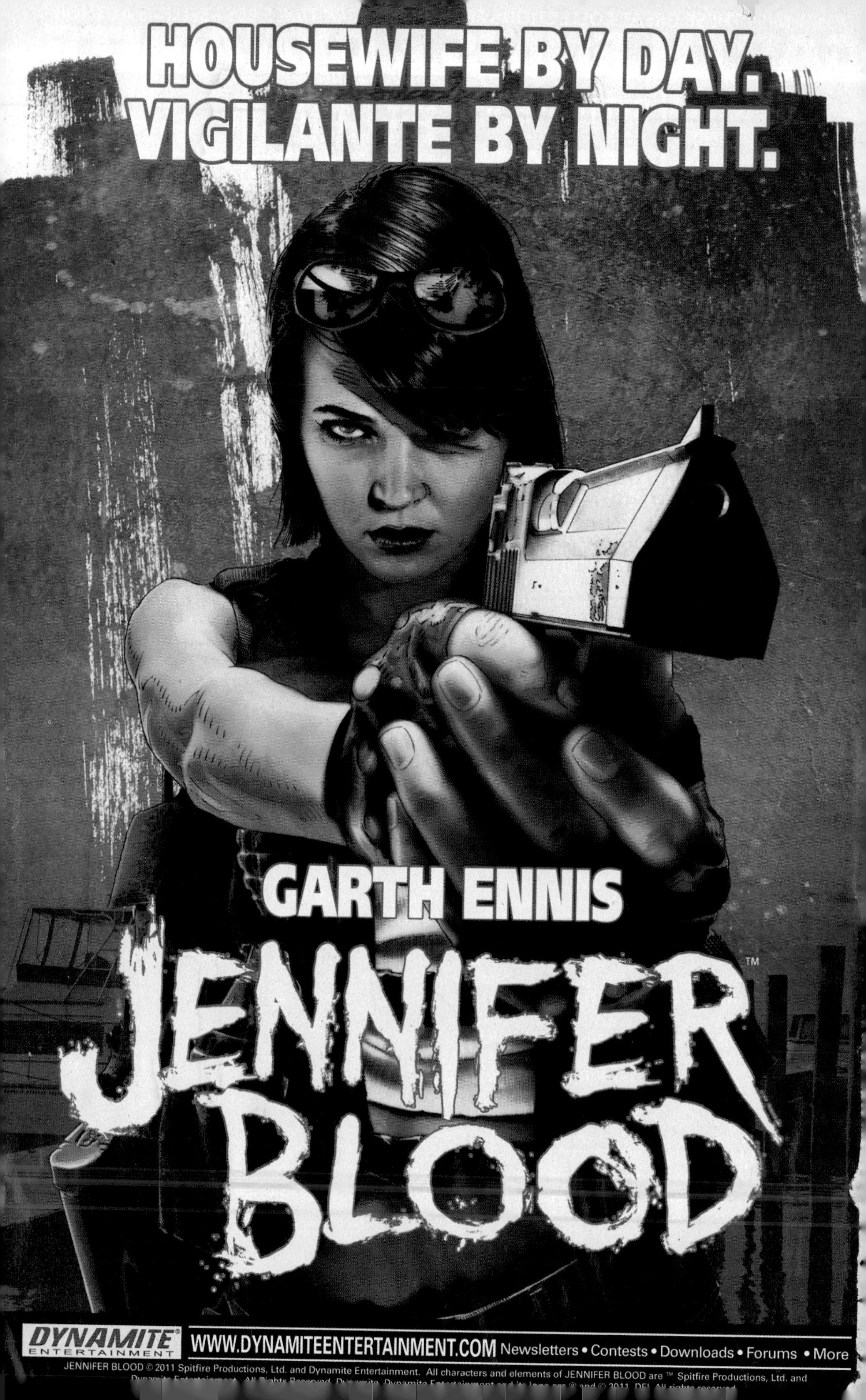

HOUSEWIFE BY DAY.
VIGILANTE BY NIGHT.
GARTH ENNIS
JENNIFER BLOOD™
DYNAMITE® ENTERTAINMENT
WWW.DYNAMITEENTERTAINMENT.COM Newsletters • Contests • Downloads • Forums • More
JENNIFER BLOOD © 2011 Spitfire Productions, Ltd. and Dynamite Entertainment. All characters and elements of JENNIFER BLOOD are ™ Spitfire Productions, Ltd. and